THE MBABZI STORY

Celebrating 100 years in Malawi

Alexandra Barron

© Alexandra Barron, 2013

Published by Alexandra Barron

Reprinted 2014

All rights reserved. No part of this book may be reproduced, adapted, stored in a retrieval system or transmitted by any means, electronic, mechanical, photocopying, or otherwise without the prior written permission of the author.

The rights of author name to be identified as the author of this work have been asserted in accordance with the Copyright, Designs and Patents Act 1988.

A CIP catalogue record for this book is available from the British Library.

ISBN 978-0-9926475-0-6

Book layout and cover design by Clare Brayshaw

Prepared and printed by:

York Publishing Services Ltd
64 Hallfield Road
Layerthorpe
York YO31 7ZQ

Tel: 01904 431213

Website: www.yps-publishing.co.uk

This book is dedicated to the people and government of Malawi for welcoming the Barron family to live, work and prosper in the Warm Heart of Africa.

Contents

	Preface	vi
	Foreword	viii
	Map of Malawi	x
	Prologue	xi
Chapter 1	The very beginning	1
Chapter 2	The start of tobacco at Mbabzi	8
Chapter 3	Marjorie	18
Chapter 4	Bruce's childhood	21
Chapter 5	Lilongwe in the 1930s	32
Chapter 6	World War II	37
Chapter 7	Life after A.F	41
Chapter 8	Meeting Doreen	49
Chapter 9	Bruce's first year at Nyasaland	59
Chapter 10	Doreen's first time to Nyasaland	65
Chapter 11	Settling at Mbabzi	72
Chapter 12	Dinner with Dr. Banda	79
Chapter 13	Lake Nyasa	81
Chapter 14	Elizabeth and Edith	87
Chapter 15	Political tension	92
Chapter 16	Independence	100
Chapter 17	Losing land and losing friends	106
Chapter 18	The shipwreck	117
Chapter 19	The Queen, Margaret Thatcher and other VIP vistors	124
Chapter 20	Chairman of Auctions Holdings Ltd.	132
Chapter 21	Busy lives in the 1980s	138
Chapter 22	Handing over	143

Preface

It was during a dinner party that Bruce and Doreen were hosting at No.2 house, on Mbabzi Estate, when the idea of a book was once again mentioned. "Alex you just need to get on and write it", declared one of their close friends, "otherwise it will never get done". The subject of having a record of the Barrons' history in Malawi was not a new one; every now and then a passing comment was made from a friend, and even members of the family, suggesting the idea. At that dinner party, in April 2005, I decided that, yes, it *was* time to give this book a go. The following week I went to No.2 house, laptop in hand, and began the first interview session with my Papa and Gogo, Bruce and Doreen.

At the time I had just started university in England, and so working on the book was limited to the holidays when I would return to Malawi. I would walk across from No.1 to No.2 house and for most afternoons for around an hour the interviews would continue. After finishing three years as an undergraduate, I completed an MSc, which again meant the book continued to develop at a rather slow pace. I think it must have been in 2011, when I had just started working fulltime in London, that I realised the 100-year landmark of the Barrons living in

Malawi was only two years away. It created the perfect deadline. Since then the work has carried on, with the interviews continuing at Bruce and Doreen's UK home in Gerrards Cross, where I would often spend a Sunday with them going through a particular section: "Right we're going to talk about the lake today", or "let's finish off Papa's time at Oxford."

I am extremely proud that the three of us have managed to do it, and that we now have a record of how the Barrons came to be in Malawi, how Mbabzi, our home and the family business, was born, and the stories that have taken place there over the last century. The last twenty years, which tells of my father taking over the family business, is deliberately kept brief as Andrew is still very much at the forefront of his responsibilities, and feels it would be better not to indulge in too much detail about the current situation.

Aside from my grandparents who have given up endless hours to devote to interview sessions and the reading and re-reading of drafts, I would like to thank the following for their help towards the book: Andrew Naish, a colleague at my current job, and Paul Wallace, a close friend whose family history is intertwined with the Barrons, both deserve a massive thank you for the time they have put into proofreading the book. Andrew, without you there would have been far too many embarrassing grammatical errors, and Paul, thank you for writing the foreword, I cannot think of anyone more appropriate to do so. My cousin Sarah Randell, thank you for your help early on with the photos. Finally, Colin Baker, a Professor who has many publications on the history of Malawi, your input in the early days was invaluable, as was your advice towards the end.

Foreword

The story of the Barrons in Malawi began in 1913. A. F. Barron's keen sense of adventure and intrepidness inspired him to venture from Livingstone in Scotland to what was then Nyasaland. The arduous journey over oceans, land and rivers took him deep into a continent that Europeans knew of only as mysterious and alien. He could scarcely have imagined that not only would Africa become his home for life, but that he would have a profound impact on the development of Nyasaland and that the family business he would come to create would still be thriving 100 years later.

The experiences of A.F. and his wife Marjorie shed light on what life was like for Europeans living in Africa in the first half of the last century. If was often hard, and they had to make do with few of the luxuries or even basic amenities that they had grown up with in the UK.

Yet it was never dull. Adventure was always around the corner. And it seemed that whatever task they took upon themselves, they were acting as pioneers. That was certainly the case when A. F. trekked with Roy Wallace from the south of Nyasaland, where almost all European settlers lived, to the central region in search of fertile farmland. Although they did not know it then, their decision to start growing tobacco close to what is today the capital Lilongwe — but was then little more than a few huts surrounded by bush — arguably changed the course of the country's history.

By the time A.F. died in 1946, the family business, made up of 16 estates, was firmly established. But the next few decades would continue to bring many remarkable moments for the Barrons as political changes swept through Nyasaland in the run up to its independence and then Malawi under Hastings Banda's leadership. Alex's book opens up parts of the country's history that are rarely told. It captures not just the wider political goings on, but the everyday lives of people who faced situations that younger generations could barely contemplate.

As Alex writes, the future for British landowners in southern Africa is never easy to predict. But the Barrons have much to be proud of when they look back on what they have achieved in Malawi over the last 100 years and four generations.

Paul Wallace

Map of Malawi

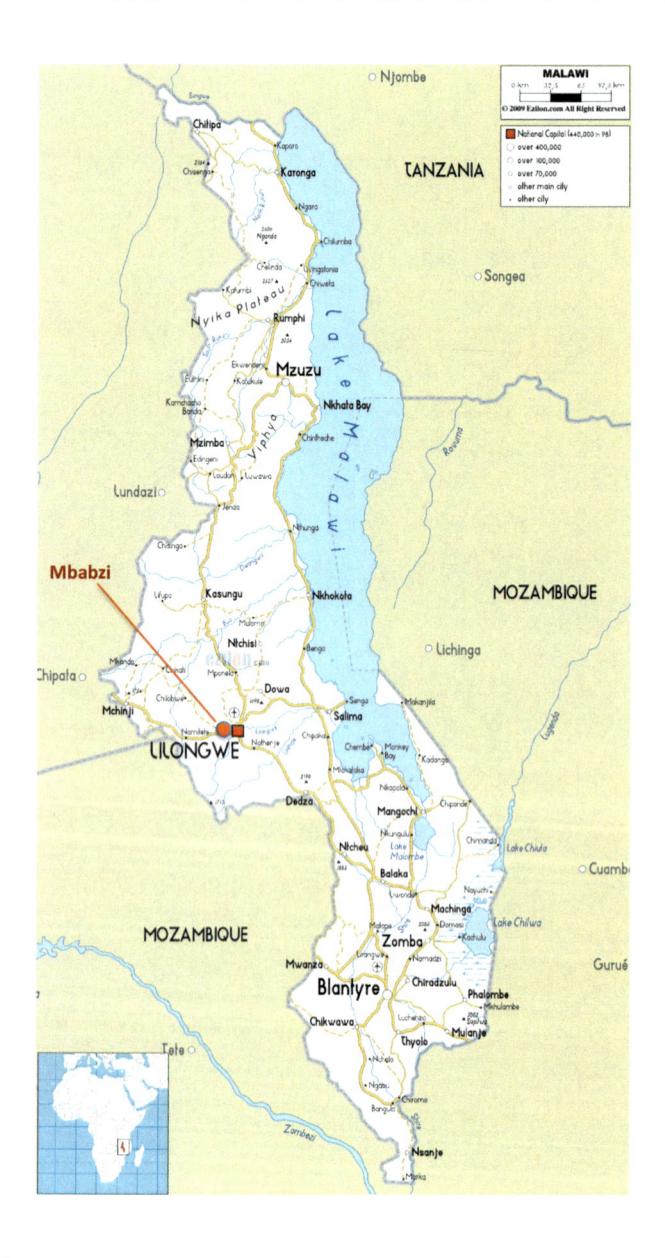

Prologue

'...with the War fought to a successful conclusion, I immediately began to think seriously of starting tobacco growing in these [Lilongwe and Dowa] areas. Many difficulties lay ahead and by no means the least of these was the fact that the market for tobacco grown in Lilongwe district was at Limbe – some 200 miles away. Two hundred miles with no railway, no motor transport facilities, and extremely poor travelling conditions during the rains, did loom up as a real obstacle, however with the "never venture never win" spirit well developed I decided to mark out land near Lilongwe and make a start, I, in conjunction with my neighbour Mr. R.W.J.Wallace.' (A.F Barron, 1919)

And so the two men, who had both been living and working in Zomba for the last six years, made the 200km journey, on foot, to Lilongwe. Upon arriving at the very small settlement, which consisted of little else aside from a few dozen Europeans, vast dense bush and scattered villages, the two men tracked down the local chief and asked if they could have some land. The chief agreed and said they could have the land between the two rivers that flowed west of Lilongwe; the Lingadzi river and the Mbabzi river. Not knowing who should have which bit of land, the men tossed a coin. Roy Wallace won the toss and chose to go by the Lingadzi river, leaving A.F with the land by the Mbabzi river. A.F liked the land he was given and decided to stay and live there. This was the decision that began the history of the Barrons at Mbabzi; a white African dynasty in Malawi, which celebrates its first centenary in 2013.

Chapter One: The Very Beginning

Bruce's father, my great-grandfather, known as "A.F" (Arthur Falconer), was born in the small town of Brechin, just north of Dundee on the east coast of Scotland, in 1893.

After finishing school, A.F studied agriculture at the University of Aberdeen. It was here he attended a lecture about the great missionary Dr. David Livingstone, a fellow Scotsman and explorer. Born in the Scottish town of Blantyre (which in the late 1800s was the name the Church of Scotland would give to a small town in southern Nyasaland – today it is the country's commercial capital), Dr. Livingstone was one of the first Europeans to travel to, and explore, the southern half of Africa in the mid-19th century. A.F was greatly inspired by Livingstone and wanted to explore this

Arthur Falconer, "A.F" Barron.

distant, foreign land for himself. To him, the idea of journeying to the other side of the world and seeing what opportunities this unknown terrain had to offer was incredibly exciting. This thirst for adventure appears to have been a Barron gene, as his older brother (one of 11 siblings!) Clarence (known as C.A) left Scotland for Africa at the same time, while one of their younger brothers, Fred, followed several years later.

So in 1913, having completed his diploma at Aberdeen, A.F set sail for Africa, aged just 20, in the hopes of work and adventure. He decided to follow Livingstone's journey to Nyasaland, a slither of land wedged between Northern Rhodesia (now Zambia), Tanganyika (Tanzania) and Portuguese-East Africa (Mozambique), a third of which was a vast expanse of water known as Lake Nyasa.

The ship sailed down the west coast of Africa, past the Cape of Good Hope at the bottom of the continent and then northwards to Beira, a small port town in Portuguese-East Africa. Upon arriving at Beira, A.F travelled north-westwards up the Zambezi river. Like Livingstone, A.F left the Zambezi where it met one of its tributaries, the Shire river, which took him north into Nyasaland. He completed the final 50 miles of his two month expedition on foot, eventually arriving at Limbe, a small town a few miles south-east of Blantyre.

A remarkable 99 years later, I am sat at No.1 house on Mbabzi Estate. I am on the *khonde* (Chichewa, the local language, for veranda) at the front of the house, which looks out on to the garden. In the middle of the garden is a statue surrounded by a low brick wall, each side of which is covered by an array of vibrant flowers. The brick wall marks what used to be a tarmac roundabout. Cars would come down the 400m driveway, and drive around the roundabout, stopping at the bottom of the concrete steps which lead up to the khonde I am sitting on. A rather regal and formal arrival for any guest, the roundabout has been replaced with flowers and a lawn. Visitors today enter the gate, and follow the drive to the left of the house where there is a much smaller, more modest roundabout. Beyond the driveway, past the trees that hide the estate from the public road which cuts through it, is a fantastic view (on a clear day) of the Dowa hills, some 40 miles away, situated halfway between Mbabzi and the lake.

The original No.1 house was made with mud and bricks. This proved to be a mistake as in the 1930s the house was invaded by termite ants, who crawled their way into the house through the mud mortar, and slowly

One of the earliest photos my grandparents have of No.1 house, pre-1933.

started to devour everything made of wood – including the window and door frames, and the timber beams that held up the roof! Before the house completely collapsed, A.F had it taken down and rebuilt. While re-building it, he inserted a sheet of flat iron into the walls, roughly three inches above the floor, which protruded about an inch each side of the wall, preventing the termites from entering. This, in the absence of any insecticides at that time, was one of the first methods used to keep termites and ants out of houses.

An aerial view of No.1 house, late 1930s.
The thatched roof has been replaced by corrugated iron. The buildings on the far left of the house were the garages, and the buildings at the top of the photograph were the staff quarters.

It is amazing to think that the structure of the house today is still the same as the post-termite invasion structure of the 1930s (we still have the flat iron sheets at the bottom of the walls in every room of the house). Aside from the interior decoration and addition of various rooms over the years, which has seen the house spread, very little has changed. The roof, which was originally thatched (and then replaced with corrugated iron in 1933/1934), still stands at a steep angle, which A.F designed to enable the rain to run down it, resulting in very high eight foot ceilings.

Above is one of the most recent photos we have of No.1 house, taken in 2010, as an 80th birthday present for my grandfather; a remarkable similarity to the previous photo taken 70 years earlier.

No.1 house was not the first place A.F lived in at Mbabzi. After the famous coin toss dictated how he and Roy Wallace would divide the land that they had found, A.F quickly built himself a little thatched shack, no more than four metres by three, in the same area where the *bwalo* ('place of work' in Chichewa), the Mbabzi office, is today. He also immediately planted a big thorn hedge around his shack to protect him from the game (elephants, lions, leopards and buffalos) that roamed the area. However, while A.F started to make Mbabzi his home, Roy chose to go back to Zomba, and employed a Mr. Walkington to look after his Lingadzi estate for him. Despite living in different parts of the country, Roy and A.F still stayed in touch, and their friendship remained very close. The friendship between the Barrons and the Wallaces has continued throughout three generations, and to this day, ten decades later, remains just as strong.

A.F met Roy during his first job in Nyasaland, where he was an assistant for A.W Boyd and T.O Thorburn on a flue-cured tobacco estate situated at Makoka, 13 miles south of Zomba. Roy was one of the few other white men working in Nyasaland and the two quickly became friends. They would often go elephant hunting together in the highlands in the central region – it is thought that A.F shot a total of 49 elephants during his lifetime! (Of course in those days big game hunting was a lot more acceptable than it is today). However, their companionship was disrupted by the First World War, which separated them for several years. As Nyasaland was a British protectorate, the country was at war with German East Africa (made up of Tanganyika (Tanzania), Burundi and Rwanda). A.F joined the Nyasaland Volunteer Reserve and was sent to fight in the north of Nyasaland (he afterwards joined the Kings African Rifles in Tanganyika), while Roy was sent to fight in France.

After the war the two men decided to travel to Lilongwe, on foot, in the hope of each establishing a home, as well as starting tobacco production in the region. On the journey from southern to central Nyasaland the men traversed a territory almost completely undeveloped and through which few white people had ever been. They were also surrounded by an abundance of game. Both keen shots, they were not going to let the opportunity go to waste and turned the trip into what was essentially a three month hunt!

I will end the chapter by quoting from an article from the *The Tobacco Revolution*, which I found in the library of the Society of Malawi, based in Zomba. I do not know the author of the article. Nonetheless, what I read was most interesting and neatly summarises the impact of the two men's decision to move to central Nyasaland:

> *'The story surrounding the division of land has become one of the tobacco legends of the Central Province… Neither of the two men could have possibly known the impact their decision would have on the future of the tobacco industry… And yet they saw for themselves, in time, the tobacco scheme they had fostered, in its broad and longer term effects revolutionized the industry.'*

Chapter Two: The Start of Tobacco at Mbabzi

Having had experience of growing flue-cured tobacco (as distinct from burley, now the most common type of tobacco in Malawi) down in Zomba, A.F decided to produce the same crop at Mbabzi. He cleared the trees and the bush, with the help of a few people from the nearby villages, and dug up the land completely by hand. The first flue-cured crop sold from Mbabzi was in 1920/1921:

'The whole of this crop – some 40 tons odd – was transported to the Imperial Tobacco Company's Factory at Limbe by tenga'tenga [the term for porters in Chichewa, being derived from 'tenga', meaning 'to bring or carry']. The nett weight carried per native was 56 lbs. and it requires little calculation to arrive at the total number of natives employed on this work[1]. *Certain natives did the journey from Lilongwe to Limbe in two weeks,*

---

1 There are 2,200 lbs to a tonne – meaning that roughly 1,571 porters were needed to transport the 40 tonne crop!

others took three, others four and some even took six weeks, but it is a definite fact, and a fact which reflects very great credit on the tengatenga, that every basket of tobacco dispatched in this manner finally reached Limbe safely. Usually up-country loads were available for the tengatenga at Blantyre, so the native thus got pay loads both ways.'
(A.F Barron, circa 1920)

While the porters, or *'tenga'tenga'*, must have experienced hardships carrying the tobacco from Mbabzi to Limbe – a distance of over 300km, much of it over rough terrain – the work provided a source of rare income for local villagers. According to *The Tobacco Revolution*, the porters were paid six shillings per trip, with a bonus of two shillings if they completed it in 14 days.

A.F, on the left, stood next to a few of the porters.

At the time that A.F was in Nyasaland there were two varieties of tobacco: flue-cured and western tobacco. A third variety, burley, was introduced later:

- Flue-cured tobacco (also known as Virginia tobacco): this was used primarily for cigarettes, and is cured, or dried, in large brick barns which are heated with metal flues

- Western tobacco, which was cured in one of two ways:

    - Dark-fired: used almost solely for pipe tobacco; dried by hanging the leaf over a small fire in a hut

    - Sun-cured: hung on a stick in a dry place indoors, then outside in the sun, alternating between the two

- Burley: dried in an open air barn (air-cured)

A.F only grew flue-cured tobacco for two years, switching to dark-fired tobacco in 1922. This was mainly because dark-fired tobacco was a lot easier to produce in the villages than flue-cured tobacco; large barns were not needed and the curing process could take place in the villagers' huts. "It was growing this type of tobacco that made A.F his reputation throughout Nyasaland," Bruce explains. Indeed this seemed to be the case, according to *The Tobacco Revolution*, which claims "it was his [A.F's] efforts, in particular, that spearheaded the growth of the dark fired industry in the Central Province".

A.F proceeded by asking local villagers to grow tobacco for him on a plot of land on his estate. He would provide them with the tobacco seed and teach them how to grow and cure the crop. The tobacco season spanned from October to April: sowing the seedbeds would take place in October, followed by planting the crop when the main rains would hopefully come in December. By March the crops would be ready for harvesting, and the leaves would then be fired-cured or sun-cured. Once the tobacco leaf had been fully cured, A.F would buy it off the villagers, usually in April, after which it would then be sorted, graded and baled, before being sent to Limbe where it was sold to the ITC, the Imperial Tobacco Company.

A.F's shed at one of the markets that were scattered throughout the area. The villagers brought the tobacco leaf in baskets, where it would be weighed and then paid for.

Using porters to move the crop did not last for long, and the following season some of the crop was transported by ox and cart. The ox and cart would travel to the Mlanda Mission, near Dedza, a small town 60 miles south of Lilongwe. From there it was taken on to Limbe by motor transport. It was not until the 1922 season that A.F dispatched tobacco to Limbe completely by motor vehicle, the first of which were two Hupmobile motor cars with trailers. Two years later the motorcars were replaced with one tonne Ford lorries which carried the tobacco to Dedza, before general transporters would deliver the crop to Limbe. This continued until the 1930s when a railway was built from Limbe to Salima and the tobacco could be transported the second half of the journey by rail. Today the crop is still transported by lorries – Mbabzi Estates owns four lorries which travel to and from Lilongwe (which is where, from 1979, the Barron's tobacco was sold).

A.F imported the very first Albion trucks into Nyasaland. Tobacco was transported from Mbabzi to Limbe on these in the 1920s. Later, the Albions were replaced by ERF lorries.

And so, by asking local people in the nearby villages to grow tobacco for him on his estate, the tenancy system was established at Mbabzi. Shortly afterwards, A.F expanded this method of production by asking the local people to grow the tobacco in their villages. Again he provided them with the seed, and would buy the crop back off them once they had grown and cured it. As dark-fired tobacco was the only cash crop available, it quickly became very popular. All the locals in the area became interested, and soon all the surrounding villages started growing tobacco for A.F and Roy. As a result, A.F started employing a large number of staff to go round the villages – by motorcycle, bike or donkey – to teach the villagers how best to grow the tobacco:

> *'It was at this juncture that I realised I must be extremely careful and put every endeavour into producing tobacco of good quality only. Production of rubbish and trashy grades – quite easily done – at this stage might have retarded, and even ruined, development entirely. It became obvious to me that as quality – not quantity – was the main factor, this could only be done by employing competent Europeans as supervisors. These Europeans continually travelled through the producing areas teaching the native producers correct methods of cultivation and of planting and curing tobacco. This was no easy task to commence with because local natives knew little or nothing about tobacco cultivation, and the whole process from seed-beds to grading and selling the cured leaf had to be taught.'* (A.F, 1920s)

However, the popularity of growing tobacco in the villages soon began to spiral out of control. Illegal buyers started travelling up from Limbe and Blantyre, attempting to purchase the tobacco from the villages, having put no work or expenses into its production, therefore able to offer better prices than estate owners such as A.F who had invested in the production. Aware of this, the government attempted to assert some control by introducing a program in 1926 called the Native Tobacco Board (NTB). The aim of the NTB was to regulate the buying of dark-fired tobacco and limit it to those who were engaged in the production and growing of tobacco in the central region, i.e. the estate owners, who in those days were all Europeans (at this time there were only around a dozen estate owners in the central region).

In the late 1920s A.F acquired a few more estates in the north of the Dowa district and on the Mudi-Bua river in the Lilongwe district. These were acquired through negotiations with the local chiefs. "The chiefs were always very welcoming to new land being acquired," Bruce explains, "as it provided a source of income to the local community." The colonial government too encouraged the expansion of the estates, as it added to the development of the region.

As his estates grew, so did A.F's production:

1923/1924:	25 tons
1924/1925:	200 tons
1925/1926:	900 tons
1926/1927:	1600 tons

These figures, taken from a transcript of A.F's written in the early 1930s, demonstrate the rapid growth of tobacco production during his first few years at Mbabzi – production in the 1926/27 season was 64 times what it was just three years earlier!

Over the next few years, this growth continued, as did the number of estates that A.F owned. By the end of the 1930s, A.F was one of the country's major land owners, with 14 estates in Nyasaland totaling 30,000 acres (12,000 hectares). The following is a breakdown of how many estates were in which district:

- Lilongwe: 5
- Dowa: 3
- Kasungu: 3
- Salima: 2
- Zomba: 1

It was also at this time that A.F bought a farm in Southern Rhodesia, in Banket, a popular farming area, 70 miles north-west of Salisbury (Harare), which he asked his younger brother Fred to manage[2]. A few years later he also bought one in Fort Jameson (Chipata), just across the border from Nyasaland in Northern Rhodesia, which was called Kapara.

---

2   As previously mentioned, Fred had travelled from Scotland to join A.F at Mbabzi several years before him. After A.F's death, the farm was sold to Fred to help pay for the death duties. The family continued to run the farm until the late 1990s, when Zimbabwean President Robert Mugabe seized the farm, forcing the family to leave.

MBABZI ESTATES LIMITED
SCHEDULE OF TITLE DEEDS

FREEHOLD LAND

Estate	Deed No.	Land No.	Acres	Date Issued	Expiry Date	Current Rent	Remarks
Mbabzi	7553		290	13/10/28	--	--	

LEASEHOLD LAND

Estate	Deed No.	Land No.	Acres	Date Issued	Expiry Date	Current Rent	Remarks
Mbabzi	9827) 11193)	LE 173	1800	1/4/35	30/9/2022	£45 or 6d./acre	
Mbabzi	16398	LE 322	5.8	7/7/49	7/7/2047	£1 p.a.	Dam.
Mbabzi	23014	LE 705		21/4/58	30/9/2022	£12.10.0	Store Licence.
Chipala	10213) 11197)	LE 177	2633	1/10/36	30/9/2030	£65.16.6 or 6d./acre	
Chipala	11308	LE 188	589	1/3/37	30/9/2030	£14.14.6	
Chipala	23069	LE 706	--	8/5/58	30/9/2030	£12.10.0	Store Licence.
Chipala	24295			1/1/59	31/12/67	(£50)	Lease to L. & B.
Chipala (Luwenga)	19571	LE 566	100	1/4/56	31/3/1973	£15.0.0	
Bua	10214) 11194)	LE 178	832	1/10/36	30/9/2029	£20.16.0 or 6d./acre	
Mudi & Kasonjola	9807) 11192m)	LE 171	3079	1/4/35	30/6/2030	£38.9.9	

A copy of the title deeds for some of the estates.

A.F was not the only estate owner expanding. There was of course Roy Wallace, who at a similar time was also acquiring estates, including one along the lakeshore area which spanned a vast 20,000 acres. Other prominent estate owners in Nyasaland were Dr. I Conforzi[3] (who also had numerous estates), as well as a small group of Europeans in the Namitete region (30 miles west of Lilongwe), which included D.W.K Macpherson, amongst others. Similar to the Barrons, the Macpherson family are today still based in Namitete running their estates, while the Wallaces still have their original Makoka estate.

---

3   Dr. I Conforzi arrived in Nyasaland, from Italy, several years before A.F. He originally settled in the southern region, where he started to grow tea and tobacco, before moving up to the central region after the First World War where he bought several more estates.

By the mid 1930s A.F was an established and considerable landowner, and Mbabzi had become a large business providing a livelihood for thousands of people. His contribution to the development of tobacco production in Nyasaland was recognised in 1933 by the British government, who awarded him with an Order of the British Empire.[4]

GAZETTE EXTRAORDINARY.

The Nyasaland Government Gazette
PUBLISHED BY AUTHORITY

691: Vol. XL, No. 14]   ZOMBA, 6th June, 1933   [———

General Notice No. 184

NOTICE.

HIS MAJESTY THE KING'S BIRTHDAY, 1933.
HONOURS.

HIS Excellency the Governor has been notified by the Right Honourable the Secretary of State for the Colonies that His Majesty the King has been graciously pleased to give orders for the following appointment:—

To the Most Excellent Order of the British Empire:—
ARTHUR FALCONER BARRON, to be an Officer (Civil Division).

ZOMBA, 3rd June, 1933.   K. L. HALL,
MP 333/31 I   Chief Secretary to the Government.

The announcement of A.F's OBE in *The Nyasaland Government Gazette*, 1933.

---

4   It is also worth noting that for many years, after settling at Mbabzi, A.F. served on the Legislative Council (known as LEG.CO). Following his death, Marjorie too servied on the council for several years.

Chapter Three: Marjorie

This is what I have gathered about Marjorie, A.F's wife, from interviewing Bruce and Doreen:

Marjorie in her wedding dress, 1929.

Marjorie was English, born in Brazil to a wealthy family. She attended a convent in France – which she hated – and following that briefly went to a finishing school in Switzerland. She loved to dance and go to parties, and was a typical debutante of the late 1920s, who was presented at court. Whereas A.F was raised on a Scottish farm with eleven siblings, Marjorie had grown up in a large house in Wimbledon Common, with a live-in maid, cook, chauffeur and gardener.

A painting of Marjorie's family's house in Wimbledon Common (1944).

You might ask, as I had done when talking to Bruce and Doreen, how a lady of such description ended up in the middle of Africa and marrying a man from such a different background to her own. Bruce recalls his mother telling him how they met aboard a ship on the way to Africa in 1928; A.F had returned to Scotland the year before to visit his family and was on his way back to Nyasaland. Marjorie was accompanying her father, Norman Dickson, also on a trip to Nyasaland. Norman was the chairman of both the renowned UK engineering firm Cleveland Bridge Company and the Nyasaland Railways (one of the three main railway companies in Nyasaland at the time, the other two being the Shire Highland railways and the Trans-Zambezi railways). A typical Victorian civil engineer, Norman built railways all over the world, including Cuba, Uruguay and Siam (now Thailand). At the time A.F met Marjorie, Norman was going to Nyasaland on an inspection tour. His company had been contracted to build the Dona Ana bridge – then the longest railway bridge in the world at three kilometres – across the Zambezi, which would link Limbe to the Mozambican port of Beira (unfortunately the bridge was blown up in Mozambique's post-independence civil war and has never been fully repaired).

It is said that A.F and Marjorie fell head over heels in love with each other as soon as they met. Things moved very quickly for the couple and they married the following year, 1929, on the 29th of November in London[4]. Following the wedding Marjorie traded her luxurious lifestyle in London for an expatriate life on a tobacco farm in the middle of southern Africa.

---

4   We do not know much about the wedding – only that it was very smart, formal and attended by six former Lord Mayors!

Chapter Four: Bruce's childhood

On September the 12th 1930 Marjorie gave birth to her first child, Bruce Robert Dickson. Bruce recites his memories as Doreen and I sit with him in the living room at No.2 house, where Bruce and Doreen have lived since 1993. No.2 was built in the 1930s along with houses No.3 and No.4 to accommodate senior staff (two more houses, No.5 and No.6, were built after the Second World War). Before Bruce starts recalling his memories, Moses, a member of the house staff, brings in some tea for us, and Doreen pours us all a cup. Bruce asks where to start. Right at the beginning, I reply. Was there anything interesting about his birth? I imagine the answer to be something along the lines of Bruce being born in a very basic missionary hospital, probably in Lilongwe. I quickly learn that Bruce was not born

Bruce, a few months old, with Marjorie (1930).

21

in a hospital, but in the house of Marjorie and A.F's friends, the Storeys[5], down in Limbe. The birth of his sister Sheila three years later however, was more along the lines that I had envisaged – at a Scottish missionary hospital in Blantyre.

Early photos of Bruce and sister Sheila.

Bruce and Sheila's childhood was spent at Mbabzi. In the 1930s it was the custom of expat families, despite much of the world being in the depths of depression, to appoint white English nannies, or governesses, to live

---

5   The husband was a senior manager of the Nyasaland Railways.

in the house and help look after the children. Marjorie made no exception to the rule just because she was in Nyasaland, and had two nannies, Nurse Martin and Nurse Hayley, travel from England to look after Bruce and Sheila. Given the economic recession in Europe, with unemployment so high, being a governess in Africa was seen as an attractive option. The governesses had their own bedrooms at No.1, in one of which Bruce and Sheila's cots were kept. Not only did they look after the two children, but as there were no European schools in Lilongwe, they also acted as nursery school teachers.

A.F, Bruce and Sheila on a rickshaw.

"At the time there were several governesses throughout Nyasaland," Doreen points out. She continues to tell the story of one such governess, based in Namitete, who married one of A.F's employees, Desmond Lewis, and moved permanently to live in Nyasaland. Doreen also reveals that, as there were virtually no young toddlers for Bruce and Sheila to play with, A.F and Marjorie paid a young servant's child to play with them!

Young Bruce, A.F, Marjorie and visitors on the khonde steps at No.1 house.

Shortly after giving birth to Sheila, in 1933, No.1 house was invaded by termites and had to be pulled down, so Marjorie took the two children to England and stayed at her Wimbledon home while the one at Mbabzi was rebuilt. The newly built No.1 house contained all the changes that Marjorie had insisted on upon arriving at Mbabzi shortly after being married. Having been used to her large house in Wimbledon, and all the luxuries it included, living with the basic amenities on offer in Nyasaland was a terrible shock for her. She quickly asked A.F for a cement floor (to replace the brick one) to be put in the sitting room and for a proper bath to replace the galvanized iron one. She was promptly given both as Christmas presents. She also planted some trees to the left hand side of the drive, which soon developed into an orchard. A.F built a series of brick channels from the water tank to the orchard to keep the trees and plants sufficiently watered. The orchard lasted many years, but was replaced with stables and a riding school when Andrew (A.F's grandson) and his wife Sheila moved to No.1 house in 1994.

The newly built house contained an impressive 24 rooms as well as three or four garages to park their cars. In addition to the house, A.F also had a tennis court built, some 200m away from the house. The tennis court is still here today and, with the exception of when the courts get flooded in the rainy season, is frequently used by the family during the holidays.

View of No.1 house with the newly built tennis court (1930s).

Visitors on the No.1 house khonde.

The new house had a large number of staff to keep it running. Bruce recites the employees and their positions.

Senior members of staff, all of whom had assistants included:

- Sani, the head servant
- Marco, who looked after the bedrooms
- Laison, head of the dining room
- The cook ("Unfortunately we can't remember his name!")

Others:

- A laundry man (known as the *dhobi*)
- A pantry man (who did all the washing up)
- A kitchen boy

- A young lad who did odd jobs, such as looking after the dogs (four or five Ridgebacks and Great Danes)
- Two *mlondas* (Chichewa for watchmen/guards)

Three members of staff in their khansu.

More members of staff.

A rather extensive list, Doreen describes how all the staff would wear *khansu*, a long robe-like uniform which came down to the ankles. They would wear white uniform for formal occasions and khaki for everyday use.

The most significant addition to the new house was a generator, which would have been imported either from England or South Africa in the 1930s. It was kept in an engine room next to the garages. It is thought that the Barrons were the first people to have electricity in the whole of Lilongwe (other European households still had pressure lamps). This attracted many guests, including the Governor, who would often stay with them when he travelled to Lilongwe from Zomba in the south (which at the time was the capital of Nyasaland).

When the new house was finished, Marjorie returned back to Nyasaland with Bruce and Sheila. However the children did not stay in Nyasaland for long, as there were pretty much no schooling opportunities for European children. A.F and Marjorie therefore made the decision to send both children to boarding school. Bruce, aged just seven, was sent back to England to become a boarder at High Trees School, in Horley, Surrey. Sheila joined him a year later.

They were only there for a couple of years, as the onset of the Second World War – and the danger of the school being bombed, given its proximity to London – led to the entire school being evacuated to Woolacombe in Devon. Sheila stayed at Woolacombe, while Bruce moved onto Rose Hill Preparatory School, in Tetbury, Gloucestershire. Astonishingly, 72 years later, another Barron, my younger sister Suzie, was also at Woolacombe School, where she spent her first year as a qualified teacher.

Despite this being the second school for both Bruce and Sheila in the space of a few years, with the war getting increasingly dangerous A.F and Marjorie decided to bring them both back to Africa. This would have been their first journey home in three years. The journey from England to Nyasaland took so long that Bruce and Sheila would normally spend their holidays in England with their grandmother, Marjorie's mother, Anne Dickson, at her spacious house in Wimbledon Common.

Bruce remembers that journey back to Africa, aboard the Warwick Castle, which set sail from Southampton and journeyed to South Africa. He describes how there were hundreds of other children, all escaping the war, and all being looked after by stewards. He remembers sleeping in bunk beds in cabins, with 3 or 4 children per cabin. The journey took longer than usual – a total of six weeks – as rather than sailing south down the west coast of Africa in a straight line, the ship had to zig-zag its way down, sometimes going quite close to South America, to try and avoid being torpedoed by submarines. Bruce recalls how on the ship's return journey to England the zig-zagging approach failed and the ship was torpedoed and sunk by the Germans; All lives on board were lost. "Thank god it wasn't the other way round," exclaims Doreen, "otherwise there wouldn't have been much of a book to write!"

Marjorie met the children in Cape Town and they continued the journey to Nyasaland predominantly by train. Once in Nyasaland, they took a car to Mbabzi, from Limbe, which took two days (and involved an overnight stay at a hotel in Dedza. I think of all the times my siblings and I complained about the long trip back from Malawi to boarding school at the end of the holidays, it was usually a three hour flight to Johannesburg, a four hour stay at the airport, and a nine hour flight to London. Door-to-door, it usually took around 22 hours. It is incredible to compare that journey with the five weeks it took Bruce and Sheila (who were both under the age of ten!).

The following September Bruce and Sheila were sent back to boarding school, this time in Johannesburg, South Africa. Bruce went to Park Town School, which at the time was an all white, or 'Europeans only', school. Similarly, Sheila's school, St. Andrews, did not allow black or Asian children. In 1944, when Bruce was 13 years old, he moved to Hilton – again a whites-only private school – in rural Natal, followed by Sheila who enrolled at St. Anne's, which was located in the same area.

To get there from Nyasaland took a tiring five days, on five different trains going across five countries! Together with other children from Nyasaland who were also going to boarding school, they would board the first train on a Saturday night at Salima, and would arrive at Limbe station on the following day. "To add a bit of colouring to this bit," Bruce says, he explains how at the last stage of the journey into Limbe, with the train travelling so slowly up the escarpment just before the town, several of the boys would jump out and walk alongside it. It travelled so slowly that they could easily keep up with its speed! From Limbe they would take a train to Beira in Portuguese East Africa (Mozambique), then another to Salisbury and then go on to Bulawayo in Southern Rhodesia. From here they would board another train which took them through Bechuanaland (Botswana), where they changed trains yet again in Johannesburg. The last and final train was from Johannesburg to rural Natal. Quite a journey! Plenty of time, as Bruce reveals, to have a cheeky smoke and an alcoholic drink along the way!

Chapter Five: Lilongwe in the 1930s

Today, if you drive into the part of Lilongwe known as Old Town there is a long stretch of road which has seen an abundance of development either side of it: there are two hotels, five petrol stations, five or six banks, a police station, at least five supermarkets, and dozens of other small shops ranging from a butchers to a stationers to bookshops. There are two sets of traffic lights and there is always a chaotic mass of traffic. This area was the main hub of Lilongwe until the 1970s, when the government decided to move the capital from Zomba to Lilongwe, and created a new central business area called Capital City, approximately 5km east of Old Town.

Back in the 1930s Old Town was the whole of Lilongwe. The long stretch of road was less than half of what it is today. It was a small strip of tar that started where the Lilongwe Hotel is and ended by the Lilongwe river. Surrounded by trees and bush, there were very few houses or buildings to be seen; the entire area was still very much elephant-hunting land with ample wildlife. The road consisted of the Lilongwe Hotel, a garage situated across the road from the hotel, a police station, a vet, an agriculture office, the Lilongwe post office, the treasury offices and a few government buildings. The government houses, which included the district and provisional commissioners' residences, were situated near where the Lilongwe Golf Club is today (at the time it was just bush).

Across the Lilongwe river there were a few Indian shops – then the only area Indians were allowed to build on. Lilongwe also included three small general stores: 'LTC' (the Limbe Trading Company), 'Kandodo' and 'Mandala'.

Kandodo was owned by the London and Blantyre Company. The first manager used a walking stick, which in Chichewa is known as an 'ndodo', from which its store name was derived. Similarly, the manager of Mandala, which was owned by the African Lakes Corporation (one of the oldest trading companies in the region, operating throughout the Southern African region), was known for wearing spectacles, the Chichewa word for which is the name of the store. The stores were basic brick buildings, with no windows. They would have a counter running along the entire length of the room, with shelves behind it stocking the goods (refrigerated goods were kept in paraffin fridges). The shops sold tinned food such as baked beans, corned beef and sardines, as well as cloth, needles, groceries and soap. Butter and bread were homemade, as there was no dairy or baking industry to speak of and other items, such as clothes and sugar, were imported from neighbouring countries, or South Africa.

Apart from these few stores and buildings, Lilongwe consisted of very little else. All the other 'areas' around

Marjorie leaving the Lilongwe post office, 1930s

present-day Lilongwe, including Capital City, were bush and a few scattered villages.

Two big developments took place in the 1930s. One of these was the creation of a nine-hole golf course (today it remains the only one in Lilongwe and the only 18-hole course in the whole country). It was built by A.F as a rather generous wedding present to Marjorie. Prior to meeting Marjorie, A.F had never played golf. But Marjorie was a keen golfer, so A.F followed her steps and took lessons in England. He enjoyed it so much he bought the land from the government and built a 9-hole golf course with sand greens. The Golf Club was run by so-called Presidents, now known as Chairmen (the name was changed because Malawi's first head of state, Dr. Kamuzu Banda, said that there should only be one person in the country referred to as a President, and that was himself). The club's first President was the PC, the provincial commissioner, followed by A.F, who replaced him a year later. A.F remained President for seven years. Many years later, A.F's daughter Sheila served on the committee and became the first, and to date the only female chairman the club has ever had.

All money made through golf fees went towards paying for the watchmen and upkeep of the course. The club soon became a social hub where Europeans in Lilongwe would meet. In the following years tennis courts were built, and after the war, playing fields were also added to the development.

The nine-hole Lilongwe Golf Club in the 1930s

The second major development was the building of Lilongwe's first airport. The first plane landed on the 4th of April 1934. The airport consisted of a single landing strip, built near what is now the Likuni road, which at the time was a route leading out of Lilongwe towards the long-established Likuni catholic mission and school. The second landing strip was built just after the Second World War. This was Nyasaland's first official airport (it was built on the edge of Lilongwe, near the present Mchinji roundabout and what is now a dense residential area, known as Area 9).

The airport consisted of a single room with a desk, scales for weighing luggage, and a little office. Small planes (Cessnas and De Havilland Beavers), holding three or four passengers, flew from Lilongwe to Limbe, Blantyre, Fort Jameson (now known as Chipata, a small town on the eastern border of Zambia), Salima (on Lake Nyasa) and Karonga in the north.

Chapter Six: World War II

As World War II broke out, A.F and others of the same generation were asked by the colonial government not to join the forces, but instead to keep the estates running, while younger men, such as Desmond Lewis (one of the first managers of A.F's estate along the Mudi-Bua river), were sent off to fight. Cigarettes were deemed a necessity for the Allied troops, so the tobacco estates in Nyasaland were operating flat out. A.F was still growing mainly dark-fired and, to a lesser extent, flue-cured tobacco. But he had also started growing a little burley. Bruce explains that burley has a mild flavour and aroma and is often mixed with Virginia flue-cured tobacco in cigarettes. The start of A.F's burley production was about the same time as the advent of the filter tip cigarette. It was also around this time that Philip Morris' Marlboro cigarettes and other brands were becoming popular worldwide, the result being a surge in demand for burley tobacco.

While the war period gave British estate owners such as A.F a good opportunity to increase yields and productivity on their estates, it was a very different situation for the Italian community in Nyasaland. As soon as Italy joined the war against Britain in 1940, the government in Nyasaland confiscated all the Italian estates, of which there were about a dozen, including all the Conforzi tea estates plus the tobacco estates in the central region. The managers were detained in a holding place, which after housing a group of Italians became to be known as 'Macaroni Castle', situated just north of Limbe on the Limbe-Zomba road.

The only Italians who were not kept in custody were the Conforzi family, as Dr. Conforzi was the equivalent of an honorary Italian Consul, and was therefore treated like an ambassador and was allowed to leave Nyasaland. At the time, one of the Conforzi tobacco estates, based in Namitete, was being run by a British man called Frank Widdas (who had come to Nyasaland, from London, seeking employment). After confiscating the Italian estates, the government approached Frank and asked him to move to Lilongwe to run the other confiscated Italian estates in the central region. Frank obliged and for the following five years he managed all the Conforzi estates.

Once the Italians had been released from Macaroni Castle, after what Bruce thinks was for about a year, and because the British government took leniency on them, they all managed to find jobs (they could not farm their own estates, as those were still confiscated and being run by Frank). One of the Italians who had been detained was Rolando Costantini, who was given work at Mbabzi, managing all the lorries and farming equipment. Rolando lived at No.4 house and worked at Mbabzi for the next five years, up until the war ended. Following this, he and his brother, Feruccio, rather than go back to work on their estates, which were returned after the war, set up the Costantini garage in Lilongwe. This still exists today, and is currently owned by Linda and Anna, Rolando's daughters, and their husbands Alberto and Eugenio. A.F and Ronaldo worked well together and became friends. This friendship between the two families has continued over the years, and, to this day, the Costantinis are close friends of the Barrons.

After the war, all the Conforzi estates were given back to Dr. Conforzi, who returned to Nyasaland to live in Thyolo, in the southern region. As a thank you to Frank for successfully running the estates during the war, Dr. Conforzi gave him the Namitete estate, which Frank had managed prior to the war.

Although A.F was not sent to fight in the war, one of his brothers-in-law, Alec Dickson, joined up in England. He was sent to Africa with a publicity unit to travel through many of the countries, including Nyasaland and Southern and Northern Rhodesia, to gain support for the King's African Rifles. The publicity unit would show communities films and documentaries about the regiment and what the King's African Rifles did, and to try to recruit soldiers. During the unit's time in Nyasaland the soldiers camped on the large lawn outside No.1 house (if you turn left out of the khonde on No.1 house, walk across the garden and through the side gate, you reach the lawn), with tents and army lorries, before they moved northwards to Tanganyika (Tanzania) in 1942.

The most interesting fact that I learnt about Alec was that he was subsequently the founder of Voluntary

Services Overseas (VSO) which he set up in 1958. VSO today claims to be "the world's leading independent international development organisation that works through volunteers to fight poverty in developing countries." It is fitting that the founder of VSO still has family in Malawi, as a few years ago, during a drinks evening I attended at the British High Commissioner's house in Lilongwe, the interim VSO country director, Anne Wuitjs was there. One of the pieces of information I will always remember in her welcoming speech was that there were more VSOs in Malawi than anywhere else in the world!

After leaving VSO, in the 1960s, Alec founded another volunteer service — Community Service Volunteers (CSV), a charity which provided those in the UK who were unable to volunteer abroad for two years (the standard period for VSO) a chance to help with projects within the UK. Perhaps the most remarkable part of this story is that through setting up VSO, Alec influenced the birth of the Peace Corps in the US. Bruce informs me that President John Kennedy had heard about VSO and sent for Alec, who flew to America to inform and advise the President about the organisation. Based on that meeting, America set up their own version of VSO, and the Peace Corps was born! For more information about Alec and his life you can read his biography (written by his wife Mora), '*A Chance to Serve*'.

Chapter Seven: Life after A.F

It was two years after the war when Bruce, who was still schooling at Hilton College in South Africa, was summoned to see the Headmaster: "I am very sorry, but your father has died."

A.F had cancer of the stomach. In September 1946 he and Marjorie travelled down to Johannesburg to seek medical attention, and it was the following month that he died. He was buried in Johannesburg. Marjorie attended the funeral alone, which must have been very difficult for her. Several weeks later, upon returning to Nyasaland, she was swamped with letters from friends and chiefs offering their condolences. Below are snippets from the *Nyasaland Times* about A.F:

> **Obituary**
> **Arthur Falconer Barron**
> It is with profound regret that the news was received in Nyasaland on Saturday of the death that morning of Arthur Falconer Barron, in hospital in Johannesburg.

> **Late A. F. Barron**
>
> One of the most enthusiastic sponsors of this sporting and social amalgamation between Lilongwe and Fort Jameson was the late Mr. A. F. Barron, and there was a feeling of sadness in the hearts of us all that he was not with us. His death has left a gap in numerous spheres in the country, many of them of far greater importance than sport and good fellowship; but it will be some time before the members of Lilongwe Golf Club will be able to realize that "A.F.", who "fathered" the Club and seemed such a part of it, has gone. A fitting tribute to his memory will be the carrying on of Lilongwe Golf Club as he would have had it — not only as the place one goes for one's sport or takes one's party to a dance, but the place where A. F.'s own spirit of friendliness and comradeship for all will prevail, and where loneliness and depression will always find an antidote, or high spirits an outlet.

> But, quite outside his direct interests, he worked hard and earnestly and left his mark on the political life of the Protectorate

> Though not one of the earliest settlers, it will be readily conceded that "A. F." for many years, right up to the time of his death, had been one of the driving forces in Nyasaland and played a major part in its development. This was recognised several years ago by the Imperial Government with the O.B.E.

> His main interest centred, of course, in tobacco — in tobacco production in general and the tobacco of the North in particular. In fact he may with complete justice be named "Father of the Native Tobacco Industry," and his enduring memorial will rightly be a well organised and prosperous peasant industry for thousands of Nyasaland Africans.

> He was the "host of hosts," as the many guests who were entertained at his beautiful home on Mbabzi Estate will remember.

The next period of Marjorie's life really demonstrates what a strong, capable and determined lady she was. A.F's death had left her with all 16 estates:

- Mbabzi, Chipala, Bua, Mudi and Kasonjola, in the west of the Lilongwe district

- Nakondwa and Chikombe, in the Salima district

- Mpale, Nkonde and Monjesi (in the Dowa district)

- Katondo, Chasinga and Nkandaula, three small estates the combination of which was about 2,000 acres, across the Bua river in the Santhe part of the Kasungu district

- Makoka in Zomba (in the same area as the Wallace's Makoka estate)

- Kapara in Fort Jameson, Northern Rhodesia

- A half share in the Gomo estate in Rhodesia (shared with A.F's brother Fred)

Her major decision was what to do with them. Was she to sell them or close them down? Marjorie was under great pressure not to continue running them by herself as she did not have the necessary knowledge or expertise to run such an expanse of estates, as well as the fact that she was a woman. In particular, the ITC (Imperial Tobacco Company), which had been buying tobacco from Mbabzi for as long as Mbabzi had existed, put great pressure on Marjorie to sell. Up until this point, Marjorie had been very friendly with the company, particularly with the senior general manager in Limbe, and the visiting directors from Bristol, who would stay at Mbabzi on their visits to Nyasaland.

The Standard Bank of South Africa — the only bank in Lilongwe at the time, of which Mbabzi was a big customer — also advised Marjorie not to take the risk of continuing to run the estates, and even her brother-in-law Fred put pressure on her to sell all the land.

Marjorie turned to John Foot[6] for advice. John had been working as a general manager at Mbabzi for the last seven or so years, having previously worked as an estate manager at Mpale, one of A.F's estates in the Dowa district. John's wife Enid also worked on the farm, primarily being in charge of the grading and sorting sheds, and was responsible for employing many hundreds of people during the grading season. Doreen stresses how it is important to include Enid in the book as "she was a remarkable lady, who worked very hard". Bruce and Doreen's high regard for Enid was illustrated years later, when they asked her to be the Godmother of their first child, Elizabeth.

John's view was that he was capable of running the estates on his own and was keen to do so, rather than see them sold. So between them they made the bold decision to keep the 16 estates and continue producing tobacco on all of them. John Foot would manage them while Marjorie would run the finances and the office administration. Marjorie came under a lot of criticism for this decision and was told by several people that she would not be successful in keeping the estates running.

---

6   John and Enid had three sons — Alan, Harry and George. Their second son Harry has maintained close contact with Nyasaland throughout his life; firstly through the colonial service, then, many years later (and after having worked as the bursar for the well-known private boys' school Charterhouse in Surrey), he and his son David set up the Nyika-Vwaza Trust. The Trust aims to preserve the Nyika plateau in the north of the country, where his son, and John's grand-son David, ran a horse-safari business for many years. Harry retired from the Trust in 2012.

Despite this, the two of them turned their back against the criticism and focused on the running of the estates. Fortunately for the both of them, the following few years after A.F's death saw good tobacco prices, as manufacturers slowly built up their stocks after the war. In some areas, such as Fort Jameson, these years saw a large expansion of tobacco farms.

One of the first big changes that John and Marjorie had to face came about as a result of a drought in 1949. Luckily the tobacco crop was not affected and prices at Mbazbi, and the other estates, remained decent. The maize crop however, which was, and still is today, the staple diet in Nyasaland, failed and the country suffered a major food shortage. To prevent such a famine happening again, the government set up the Maize Control Board the following year. The Maize Control Board stipulated that the majority of estates throughout Nyasaland, including Mbabzi, could become commercial buyers of both maize and groundnuts, on behalf of the Maize Control Board. Bruce recalls being told by Marjorie that this was on a commission basis, "two shillings for a bag of maize, and three shillings for a bag of groundnuts". The scheme allowed the government to build up substantial stocks of maize so that in the event of another drought there would not be such severe shortages.

The estates involved in the scheme had to provide all the money themselves. This led to dozens of little markets being set up throughout the districts, whereby growers from the villages would bring their maize and groundnuts at a fixed price to sell to the estates. The maize/groundnuts would be weighed, sewn into sacks and in due course transported into Lilongwe for storage and safekeeping. Consequently, the following years saw Mbabzi buy tens of thousands of tonnes of maize and groundnuts. The timing of this was most fortunate for John and Marjorie, as the following year, 1950, saw the tobacco prices crash (so much so that many of the estates in Fort Jameson, which had been newly opened after the war, closed down), and the same again happened in 1952. Thankfully, the maize and groundnut commissioning revenue offset the decline in tobacco prices and Mbabzi remained viable and stayed in business.

Another obstacle that John and Marjorie faced within their first years of running Mbabzi without A.F was the implementation of two rather "anti-estate" measures which were introduced by the governor, Sir Geoffrey Colby, who, as Bruce diplomatically says, "was not a friend of the estates".

The first measure that Sir Geoffrey implemented, in 1948, was the banning of all estates from buying tobacco that was not grown on the estates. This meant that villagers could only sell their tobacco straight to the African Tobacco Board (previously known as the Native Tobacco Board), rather than selling it to Mbabzi or other estate owners. As a result everything had to be produced and grown on the estate itself, and the total tobacco volume that Mbabzi could offer for sale was significantly reduced.

At a similar time, Sir Geoffrey introduced a second regulation – that all tobacco had to be sold over the auction floors to the buyers, instead of directly to one of the tobacco buying companies. Ever since A.F had first started producing tobacco, it had always been sold to the ITC and so the implementation of this rule led to the end of a long-standing association of the Barrons with the ITC. Evidence of the long-standing relationship is on show at No.1 house, where, on the mantelpiece in our dining room a silver salver is displayed. This salver, on which is written *"Presented to Marjorie Widdas By The Directors Of The Imperial Tobacco Co Ltd. 6th May 1951"*, was given to Marjorie by the ITC, to mark the end of the association, shortly after Sir Geoffrey introduced the new regulation (it also showed that the ITC's initial ill-feeling towards Marjorie's decision to hold on to the estate's after A.Fs death had waned). Selling tobacco on the auction floors rather than directly to a company made life a lot harder for Marjorie and John Foot as, similar to the situation for tobacco farmers today, they did not know what price they were going to get for their tobacco. In recent years Malawi has seen a reversion to contract-growing, especially among large landholders. The government has even talked of having as much as 80% of the country's tobacco sold via the contract system. However, most tobacco is still sold via the auction floors.

While the estates, or rather the regulation of the estates, faced significant changes, Marjorie's personal life too changed; four years after A.F's death she remarried. The man was Frank Widdas (who was mentioned earlier, he was asked by the government to run the confiscated Italian estates during the Second World War). Their marriage caused quite a bit of stir and gossip in Lilongwe, as at the time that Frank and Marjorie met, he was married to one of Marjorie's good friends! Frank left his wife, Marian, for Marjorie, and needless to say the two women's friendship came to an abrupt end.

Following the wedding, Frank moved from his estate at Namitete, to live at No.1 house at Mbabzi. Bruce explains how Frank had originally asked Marjorie to move to Namitete, but she refused as his house was far too small and primitive for her to live in. However, although he lived at Mbabzi estate, Frank made it clear that he would have nothing to do with running the business, and for the next three years he did not interfere. Instead, Frank would travel from Mbabzi back to his own estate in Namitete, where he would spend a few nights each week, and then return back to No.1 house.

Bruce describes Frank as a clever man; he was good company, cheerful and subsequently gave Bruce a lot of good advice when he later took over the running of Mbabzi. However, Marjorie and Frank's marriage did not last and in 1967 they got a divorce. Coincidentally, both of her marriages only lasted 17 years (1929-1946, 1950-1967).

Chapter Eight: Meeting Doreen

While Marjorie was getting to grips with running the estates with John Foot, and subsequently meeting and marrying Frank, Bruce had since finished school in South Africa and had moved to England, where he was accepted to study at Oxford University, in 1948 (two of Marjorie's brothers had gone to New College at Oxford University and she was keen for Bruce to go there as well).

Bruce started to read PPE (politics, philosophy and economics). "A point worth noting," Bruce says, "was that my tutor for philosophy was the late famous Isaiah Berlin, who wrote many books and memoirs including *'A life of Karl Marx'*." However, despite Professor Berlin being a clearly very intelligent academic, Bruce's memory is of him being a poor tutor: "he was so clever it was like he could not understand that I simply was not as clever as him." Although Bruce enjoyed the politics side of the degree, by the end of the first term he was failing philosophy, and was told he could no longer continue to read PPE. Luckily New College allowed him to switch to history, on the condition that he passed his exams at the end of the second term, or else he would be kicked out of the university. Bruce needed no further warnings, and from that moment on he worked extremely hard in order to pass the exams; he would attend lectures in the morning, get a cheap lunch at a "British restaurant", and would then go to the college library for the afternoon where he would study until 7pm or 8pm. The hard work paid off, and at the end of the second term Bruce passed his history exam.

THE SPECTATOR, J.

UNDERGRADUATE PAGE

Going Up

By B. R. BARRON (New College, Oxford)

UNLIKE the majority of undergraduates going up to Oxford today for the first time, I did not just catch the train at Paddington or the 'plane in New York. I well and truly "went up," as I began my journey some 13° S. of the Equator, and went right up north to the rather cooler latitude of Oxford. I was keeping up the family connections, following the family's footsteps, even though they were not the footsteps of the usual father or elder brother, but of a pair of pre-war uncles.

It all began early one Sunday morning in August with a farewell I shall always remember. As I drove away from the house for the last time, for several years at least, I noticed that a crowd was gathering at the end of the drive. Instead of the usual Sunday morning quiet, there was a growing noise. Then I saw that seven large squat Diesel lorries had been drawn up in a semi-circle facing the drive; the idea was to create as much noise as possible, and so every lorry's engine was "revved" to capacity, every hooter was blown, while a passing bullock-cart was persuaded to remain and lend local colour to the general effect. A throng of small children wildly beat empty petrol-tins, while over everything hung a haze of pungent blue smoke from the exhausts. Only the bullock remained impassive. It was a moving farewell; but I have yet to discover whether there was any intention behind it of accustoming me to the supposed clatter and crowd-effects of Oxford, as it existed in the imaginations of the inhabitants of Central Africa, or whether it was in the nature of a grand finale, since my next three years would be spent in quiet contemplation and sober study.

All that day we motored the two hundred and thirty miles to the first stop. My companions were my mother and a houseboy's wife going to have her tonsils removed. There were no mishaps, and we dustily arrived. The next day I changed my mode of transport to a small and staid Rapide biplane, which carried me slowly over the four hundred miles to Salisbury. It flew over hundreds of square miles of characterless bush, mostly owned by Portugal. The Zambesi River, the one great landmark on the trip, was visible for half an hour before we flew over it. As I looked down, I could see the tiny settlement of Tête on one of the banks, the farthest point reached by the Portuguese knight-explorers who marched up the steamy river-valley in full armour. After a four-hour flight, I landed at Salisbury and civilisation. I was now in a city of tarred roads, of plate-glass shop-windows, of two-storeyed houses and buses, all of which were lacking in my own neighbourhood. Salisbury was an important stage in going up. Here I expected to collect my luggage, which had had to be sent by road a fortnight earlier; and here, as if by a miracle, I did find it.

I entrained for Johannesburg, once again changing my mode of transport. Johannesburg was forty-eight hours' travel away, half of them through the Kalahari desert. All along the line in the Kalahari the natives tried to sell us hideous wooden animals, scorched to give them colour and with none-too-clean rabbit-fur glued on in the appropriate places. They also, and more successfully, tried to sell us lovely little table-mats and necklaces of stone beads. The whole of one day was spent in the long climb to Johannesburg, six thousand feet up. The train pulled slowly across the high veld, rolling plains with little towns scattered over them. These towns were almost exact replicas of every Wild West cinema town. Opposite the station there was usually a hotel, with horses tied to the railings, and there would be one dusty main street, one big store, while opposite the platform would be some corrals filled with long-horned cattle.

If Salisbury was civilisation, Johannesburg was "this modern age." There is all the rush and noise of a modern city, especially an American one, in Johannesburg. There are lofty buildings, juke-boxes, cars with too much chromium plating on them and not enough space in which to park. The hotels are lit by invisible fluorescent lighting, whereas in Salisbury we had to do with plain

ANUARY 20, 1950

electric bulbs. I caught the Blue Train to Cape Town. It is South Africa's luxury train, and possibly the only train in Africa that averages more than 35 m.p.h. for any distance.

I arrived at Cape Town, the second important stage in my journey to Oxford, for here I caught the boat. I was quitting the land of many servants, and I believed I was going to a country of queues and cold weather. I had my last good meal, so I thought; one that seemed fit for any Elizabethan traveller. Perhaps the first thing I observed on board ship was that all notices were in one language. All the way to Cape Town they had been in Afrikaans or Portuguese as well as English. It was a quiet voyage; the ship was only half-full. There were the usual ship's Derby, visit to the bridge, auction on the day's run. The passengers were pleasant and ordinary, and, as there were few of us, I was able to get to know nearly everyone, including one unfortunate boy going to Cambridge.

The ship had loaded its supplies in England or else was under the Ministry of Food, for we had our one-egg-a-week ration, a great surprise to most on their first breakfast. I thought that my worst forebodings were realised about England, and I conjured up visions of a hungry student for ever thinking of food when not of his work. One morning in September I awoke and heard the unusual but expected sounds of the docks, and I knew I had nearly reached the journey's end. It was the point where I picked up my uncles' footsteps; they always went up from London, so to London I went.

I gazed avidly at the, to me, famous English countryside, the lovely greenness of it all, the flatness and the freshness. I saw the unusual hedges; I felt the greater speed of the trains; I heard the unfamiliar accents. But the most striking aspect of England was the rows and rows of chimney-pots. The nearest thing to them I had ever seen was on a Nature study film at school showing hundreds of swallows resting on telegraph wires. Then I reached Waterloo, where I met my relations (but not my uncles). I passed a few days in London, which seemed a far more peaceful city than Johannesburg or Cape Town. I saw my first play, *Oklahoma*, and travelled on my first Tube train, both of which gave me enormous pleasure. I dutifully saw the sights of London; I visited the famous places, and then one day I realised I had nearly arrived. I was almost up, for I found myself at Paddington asking for "a third single to Oxford, please."

> I no longer felt I was going up, but going along. I seemed to be coasting down a well-worn path which so many thousands of others had followed before me—including my uncles. The journey quickly slipped past, while I dreamed about what I was coming to and the end of my travels. Outside the countryside was looking grey and damp, covered with a faint mist, but still retaining much of the pleasantness of what is new and fresh. Then suddenly I saw Oxford, the Oxford of the past, with its towers and steeples, turrets and battlements, looking like an unmade jig-saw puzzle. But it was soon obscured by the Oxford of the present, by rows of small houses, by the gasworks and goods yards.
>
> I ended as I began, in a car, which drove slowly through the town with its strange mixture of the old and new, with the ancient colleges on one side of a street and modern shops on the other. Everywhere there were bicycles, also old and new, but mostly very old, and which seemed to have an unofficial right-of-way. Then I turned down a narrow, walled-in lane and stopped before the great college gates, through which I could glimpse patches of green through the piled-up trunks in the lodge. I stepped out of the car, through the gates and into a new life. I was up.

An article written by Bruce about his journey from Nyasaland to Oxford, which was printed in *The Spectator*, 1950.

It seemed that choosing to switch to history had been a wise decision, from a student's perspective, as that was the only exam of the whole course, until his finals at the end of the third year, and so for the rest of his time at university Bruce enjoyed himself immensely. He was in the college First Eleven hockey team, the college tennis team, and during his holidays would often venture to France. But I suspect the reason that he found university so enjoyable was that it was around this time that he met Doreen Richardson.

I love hearing the story of how the two of them met: it was in December 1950 at the English Speaking Union on Charles Street in London. Doreen told me how she would frequently go there to go Scottish dancing with a couple of girlfriends. Born in Lincolnshire, and the youngest of four, Doreen was from a middle class background, where her father ran a small motor engineering business. She moved to London in 1947, aged 19, to complete a secretarial course at *Mrs. Hosters*, in Grosvenor Place, having failed to get in to university. Soon after completing the course she found secretarial work at the Colonial Development Cooperation (later to become the Commonwealth Development Cooperation). She tells me of how, much like myself, she adored living in London; she and her friends went to theatres, operas, the ballet, and she was a member of the Ealing tennis club. On that particular night at the English Speaking Union, Doreen was sitting down watching her two girlfriends dance, when a nice young man, who was "slightly film-star looking with lovely fair hair", came up to her and asked if she would join him in a dance. Doreen agreed and they started talking. Naturally Doreen asked the question of where Bruce was from. Unlike a lot of other people, Doreen had heard of Nyasaland through her job. They spent the evening chatting, and agreed to meet again. Little did Doreen know then, that meeting this man at the English Speaking Union in the heart of London, would lead to her moving her entire life to the middle of Africa, where she would live for the next fifty years.

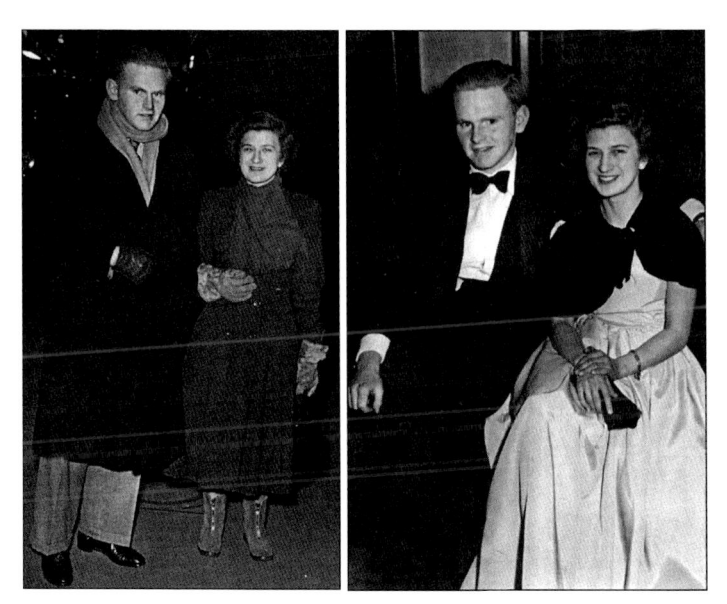

Early photos of Bruce and Doreen, early 1950s.

Another one of the stories of when Bruce and Doreen first met that Doreen loves to tell me is of their first New Year's Eve celebration together. Doreen had been planning to be with her mother and sister in Lincoln for it, but Bruce was keen to spend it with her and so invited her to London. He casually mentioned that he might be able to get tickets for the Chelsea Art Ball, which was held at the Royal Albert Hall. Doreen was ecstatic; it was every young lady's dream to go to the prestigious and glamorous Chelsea Arts Ball and she quickly told all her girlfriends about it. However, a few days before the ball, Doreen received a phone call from a rather bashful Bruce revealing that he didn't actually have any tickets – it was merely a ploy to get her to come to London to spend New Year's Eve with him. Having made no plans, he asked if he could go with her to the Ealing tennis club instead. "Despite not being able to go the ball we still had a great New Year's Eve together," Doreen explains.

Over the next two years, Bruce and Doreen's relationship blossomed and they had many wonderful occasions together. During term time Doreen would go and visit Bruce in Oxford, where they would meet up with their long-standing friends, Greta and Tony Malein. Greta is an old school friend of Doreen's; they met when they were both 15 years old, and to this day remain great friends! Bruce would also visit Doreen in London where they would go to the Lyons Corner House, "the cheapest eating place in London", or the Queen's tennis club where Bruce was a member – and undergraduates were offered special rates, Bruce adds. The following Easter Bruce asked Doreen to go to Paris with him, and a few months after that he asked her to the May Commemoration Ball at Oxford, a very prestigious event. "It was glorious," explains Doreen, "all the men wore white ties and tailcoats – Bruce hired his – there was champagne being handed round by waiters, and there were two brass bands."

After finishing his degree (narrowly missing getting a First), Bruce completed a Pitman Secretary/Business course in London, in the hopes of becoming a journalist. However, this ambition was short-lived, as Bruce quickly found he would be very unlikely to find work – particularly as one of his close friends from Oxford, whose brother was the art editor of the famous *Tatler* magazine, was struggling to find work – even with his family connection! Bruce therefore made the decision to go back to Nyasaland and start work at Mbabzi.

I should mention at this point that although Bruce had made the decision to return to Mbabzi and take over the family business, our neighbouring farm, Lingadzi, owned by the Wallaces, was still being run by Roy. "Roy was so good to us, a very very helpful man." Bruce remarks. It was only in the mid-1960s that Roy's son, Simon, took over the running of Lingadzi from him. And just as A.F and Roy had been close, so were Simon and Bruce, as was Simon with Bruce's son Andrew (and subsequently Andrew's children with Simon's children).

Between making this decision to work at Mbabzi and leaving England to return back home, Bruce asked Doreen to marry him and on February the 6th 1952, their engagement was announced. The timing was somewhat unfortunate as it was the same day that King George VI died, and was a day of national mourning. This naturally put a bit of a damper on their celebrations, especially as most places closed for the day. Despite this, Bruce and Doreen met up with two mutual friends and celebrated the engagement at the nightclub Ciros before going on to the famous Café de Paris. The following day the whole family went out shopping in Kensington High Street, with Doreen suffering from the only hangover she thinks she's ever had – a result of drinking brandy and Benedictine!

The blissful period of being a recently engaged couple, however, was short-lived, as soon after the engagement Bruce had to return to Mbabzi to start his career. Unbelievably, the next time that Bruce and Doreen would see each other would be in July 1953 – with Doreen being apart from her new fiancé for 18 months! They kept in touch through consistently writing letters to each other

– only means of communicating. I ask Doreen how she managed over the 18 months, imagining it to have been an incredibly tough and trying time for her to be kept away from her partner for so long. But, despite missing Bruce terribly, Doreen says she managed to have a good time and enjoy herself; she loved London, had lots of friends, and was very social, whether that was at the tennis club, going to the theatre or Scottish dancing. I delicately ask if, while being separated from Bruce for over a year, there were any temptations along the way... "There was once a medical student who asked me to go to a dance at the English Speaking Union," she explains. Unsure what to do she rang up Bruce's grandmother, Anne Dickson, for advice. Anne recommended that Doreen did go to the dance but then come to stay at her flat in Kensington[7] at the end of the night. Doreen had a pleasant time and at the end of the night followed Bruce's grandmother's advice and took a taxi to her flat. And no, she assures me, there was never any "hokey-pokey" while Bruce was away.

---

[7] Bruce's grandmother moved from her house in Wimbledon Common to an equally luxurious flat in Kensington. The flat consisted of five or six bedrooms – one of which was used by a live-in cook. During his time at Oxford university, the Kensington flat became Brue's English home, which he would stay in frequently during the weekends and holidays.

Chapter Nine: Bruce's first year at Mbabzi

Bruce, Doreen and I are once again seated in the living room of No.2 house, ready for another interview session, when I ask him what his first memory was of going back to Mbabzi and starting his career. "Failing my driving test," Bruce replies – not quite the answer I was expecting! As with most failed first driving tests, his story is rather an amusing one; Bruce was driving slowly round one of the residential areas when he was asked by the driving instructor to reverse between two pillars of a gate. Unfortunately Bruce misjudged the distance behind him and knocked one of the gate pillars down. The gate happened to belong to the Provincial Commissioner, only the most senior government servant in the whole area! Luckily Bruce managed to make a swift exit and was not caught. He was more successful the second time, and was soon given a small car, a Hillman Minx, by Marjorie.

On a more serious note, Bruce explains how once he had settled back at Mbabzi, he spent his first month travelling round the farm with the senior African foreman – Mr. Eliot Tandwe – to learn, and pick up as much information as he could. At this time, all the tobacco, which was mainly burley and sun-cured, was still being grown on the tenant system.

From the very start Bruce loved the work, and very much enjoyed learning it from scratch from the people who worked there. There was virtually no English spoken by anyone, except the occasional clerk, so Bruce had to pick up Chichewa, which back then was known as Chinyanga, very quickly.

An aerial view of the *bwalo*, the long thin buildings to the right of the photo are the grading sheds.

After getting to grips with the basics of how the estate operated, Bruce started to work in the grading sheds. His daily routine consisted of the following: he would cycle from No.1 house to the sheds, which were located in the *bwalo,* before it was light, and where there would be several hundred people waiting to start work. Their job was to grade and sort the tobacco, bale it, and send it off to be sold. The doors to the sheds would be opened, hurricane lamps put inside the sheds to allow some light, and mats placed on the floor for the tobacco to be sorted on. During the grading season a loudspeaker system was put in the sheds, which played local music throughout the day. After the sheds had been opened and work had begun, Bruce would cycle back to No.1 house for breakfast at 8:30, going back to the sheds shortly after. A simple lunch – such as bits of chicken – would be sent to him on a tray by one of the members of staff, and later in the afternoon tea would also be sent to him. When the work was done for the day, Bruce would cycle back home. Bruce did this for five and a half days a week, from the middle of April to the middle of August, which was the buying and grading part of the season.

Tobacco barns.

During the weekends Bruce would socialise at the Golf Club with a small group of bachelors who were based in Lilongwe; he would play tennis, rugby and a bit of cricket. He would also spend his time at the Mbabzi football ground (which was built by A.F) with the Mbabzi football team. Made up of employees with a couple of outsiders from nearby villages, Bruce formed the team within his first few months of being back at Mbabzi. Between February through to April, once work had finished at 4pm, Bruce would go to the football field to help arrange the football, pick the teams and act as a referee (from April onwards football took place only at the weekends as Bruce, and most of the football team, would be working in the sheds until dusk). Bruce would announce the names of those who would play in the weekend match over the loudspeaker in the grading sheds – something he greatly enjoyed doing. Matches were held at the weekends, where Mbabzi would play against other local teams in the area, such as Chitedzi, a few miles west of Mbabzi, where the local agricultural research station is based. The football team still runs today, with Mr. Liffa, the Head of Security at Mbabzi (since 1998), in charge. The team is funded by Mbabzi Estates, and has travelled all around the central region to play against other teams. They remain a strong team and in 2006 they won the regional championships!

By the time August arrived, Bruce was sent to look after the Mudi and Kasanjola estates in the west of Lilongwe district. Mudi was about 1,000 acres and Kasanjola was about 2,000. Like at Mbabzi, both grew burley and sun-cured tobacco.

Whereas No.1 house had over a dozen rooms, the house at Mudi only had three; it was a very simple house that lacked a lot of the luxuries, such as carpets and running water, that No.1 house had. Its amenities included a paraffin pressure lamp, a paraffin fridge and a tin bath. There was also a latrine which was situated in a hut separate from the house; it consisted of a wooden box which you would sit on over a receptacle, which the watchman would then remove once you had "done your business." As Doreen says, it was "primitive in the extreme".

Up until Bruce started working at Mudi, there had been only one member of staff at the Mudi house – a watchman. When Bruce started working there, Marjorie employed a learner cook, Dailes, who would travel up to Mudi with Bruce. At the beginning of each week, Marjorie would give Bruce a box of food for that week which usually consisted of a large piece of beef, some vegetables, potatoes, bread and milk, and with that food there was a standard meal routine that Dailes would prepare for Bruce's evening meals:

- Monday: Roast beef
- Tuesday: Beef curry
- Wednesday: Beef stew
- Thursday: Beef rissoles

Bruce describes how he would spend his days. At dawn he would cycle to the little head office where he would meet the head capito (foreman), who managed the tenants and labourers. The two of them would spend the day going round and round the estates, walking up and down each tenants garden to see how they were getting on. "We would tell them things like: 'you need to weed more, you're behind with your sowing'". They would break for lunch and repeat the process in the afternoon. Bruce thinks out loud: "There were probably around 80 tenant gardens at Mudi and 160 at Kasanjola. During the space of five days we would have to visit every garden. You see how it was a very busy time for me!"

As it was all very new to Bruce he explains how he was heavily reliant on the head capito teaching him and giving him advice on how to advise the tenants. John Foot would also drive up from Mbabzi once a week to check how Bruce was getting on.

Bruce would spend his evenings reading in the sitting room by the light of the paraffin lamp – he recalls reading 'Churchill's Life of Marlborough' – and would usually be in bed by 8:30 – 9:00pm, and up by the first light. At the end of the week Bruce would drive back to Mbabzi in his Hillman Minx to spend the weekend at home socialising at the Golf Club.

Bruce lived at the house in Mudi until the end of the season, in July 1953. By this time he had been away from Doreen for over 18 months and so made his return to England, for the wedding.

Chapter Ten: Doreen's first time to Nyasaland

Between Bruce returning to London and Doreen and him moving to Nyasaland, they had their wedding. The wedding took place in Doreen's village Parish church (where she was also baptized and confirmed) outside Lincoln, in the village of North Hykeham, on the 19th September 1953. It was a small wedding with around 50 guests, "invites were sent out to 150 or so, but so many people weren't able to travel to Lincoln". Unfortunately Bruce's sister Sheila was also unable to attend as she was studying for her finals at the University of Cape Town. As Doreen's father had died several years earlier, Doreen's brother Robert gave her away. "Our friends and family greatly enjoyed the occasion and a happy time was had by all," says Doreen.

"Our married life didn't get off to the smoothest of starts", Doreen continues, "as shortly after waving goodbye to our friends, we were on the way to Grantham station when I realised I had left my brand new coat – which was part of my trousseau – behind." They had to ask the driver to turn back and retrieve it. By the time they arrived at the station they had missed the train and had to wait on the platform for the next one, alongside many of the wedding guests! Despite missing the first train they got to the airport in time to catch their scheduled flight to the Channel Islands, only to realize that their flight had been cancelled due to fog. The couple had little choice but to grudgingly head back to Doreen's flat in London – "where there was no food!" – to spend the first night of their honeymoon! Needless to say this did not put a damper on their special day, and the next morning they went back to the airport and caught a flight to Sark, where they had a "a fabulous two weeks on the beautiful island."

Shortly after the wedding Doreen had to say goodbye to not only her family and friends, but her life and home, as the two of them boarded a ship, *The Braemer Castle*, back to Nyasaland, which was to become Doreen's new home:

> *"So here was I, a girl from Lincolnshire who had been abroad only once, setting sail in 1953 for the great unknown. The journey itself took five weeks, by boat, train, plane and car. I told myself that life would be an adventure."* (excerpt from a speech made by Doreen in 2012 to the National Council of Women, Chalfont-St-Peter, UK)

Doreen recalls the journey; the ship was not luxurious, but was a one-class vessel, on which they had a basic little cabin with bunk beds. "But we met some wonderful people on board, some of whom we are still friendly with today.' The ship left Tilbury and sailed down the Thames across to Rotterdam. Doreen remembers being absolutely shocked by the devastation that they saw in

Rotterdam; the city had been completely flattened by bombs, even though this was several years after the war. Following Rotterdam the ship sailed through the Bay of Biscay, stopping at the Portuguese islands of Las Palmas, Ascension and St. Helena. From there they continued down to Cape Town.

Upon finally arriving in Cape Town, they stayed at the famous Mount Nelson hotel, whose corrugated iron roofs "made it seem old fashioned for such a famous hotel, and a little bit grubby!" Doreen remarks. "Although our room did have a wonderful view of the sea."

Doreen was grateful when the ship finally reached Cape Town as she had suffered from seasickness ("I was not used to being on a ship for such a long time"), as well as a sore throat and the first pangs of being home sick. This was only made worse when she was taken ill on the train journey from Cape Town to Bulawayo after, for drinking some bad water (unaware that one had to be careful about water in Africa!).

View of Table Mountain from the *Braemer Castle*.

A closer view of Table Mountain.

Once at Bulawayo, they continued, on train, onwards to Salisbury, which took three days. Doreen found the train ride the most tedious experience, while Bruce found it exciting as it brought back memories of travelling to and from school. The final leg of the journey into Nyasaland was by plane, straight to the Chileka airfield, in Blantyre, where they stayed a couple of nights at Ryalls hotel. The hotel, although it has been refurbished and modernised over the years, is still in the same place today and is frequently used by Andrew, Bruce and Doreen's son, on his business trips to Blantyre. Doreen was struck by how everyone knew everyone, and how friendly people were to each other. She remembers meeting Hugh Proverbs at the hotel, who at the time worked for the government in livestock husbandry (he, Bruce and Doreen have remained good friends for 56 years!), as well as another person who was, rather bizarrely, a snake expert. The following day they bought a lovely new car, a Vauxhall Velox – "which we were so proud of" – and set out for Lilongwe, going via Zomba. Doreen recalls, "after

40 miles the road narrowed and I thought we were approaching the farm, but no, this was the great north road to Lilongwe... I remember as we set off in the bush by car for my future home that people kept waving and this was when we were 200 miles away. Bruce said this was common practice and we still think it's a very friendly habit."

The car journey took twelve hours, which included a ferry crossing at the Shire river, which was pulled across on a steel cable by Malawians.

A postcard of the Shire river ferry.

Just outside Dedza Doreen experienced her first African storm (where four and a half inches of rain fell!), which made the journey even slower. The car skidded and slid about the muddy road. Bruce recalls at one point it slid backwards into a bank, breaking the tail lamp, on their new car's first journey! After driving for more than eleven hours, they eventually arrived at a little strip of tarmac, "a glorious relief from the terrible road", which was situated in the middle of a small settlement. "Welcome to Lilongwe!" Bruce exclaimed as they arrived at the tarmac, to which Doreen's reply was "Where?!" For those of you who are familiar with Lilongwe, the strip of tar went from where the Lilongwe bridge is today up to the corner of the Lilongwe Hotel. No sooner had they arrived on the tar, they were back on the dirt road again. By this time it was nearly dusk and still pouring with rain.

They soon approached the bottom of the hill that to this day still leads to the Mbabzi estate. Where there is now a school, *Mpita* Secondary School, back then there lived some Indians, including a Mr. O. A. Patel. They owned little stores that sold cloth, matches, soap, sugar, and paraffin to the local villagers. It was at this point that Bruce jokingly informed Doreen that they had arrived at Mbabzi. Doreen looked up and saw the two little stores, and thought "dear god where have I come to?" She nearly burst into tears. Luckily for Doreen, they drove up the hill, which was surrounded by complete bush (today it is surrounded by farmland) and turned onto the long gravel driveway where Bruce proudly announced they were home. By the time they arrived Doreen was practically in a state of collapse. The whole journey had taken over a month! Marjorie and Frank, who had been worried about them as the weather had been so awful, were relieved to see the car pull up, and welcomed Doreen to her new home. Despite her exhaustion and state of being overwhelmed, Doreen ends our interviewing session by stating that she had come out to Nyasaland out of love for Bruce, but also because of her love for adventure. She concludes: "The day that I set foot in Nyasaland my adventure started, and it has not stopped yet!"

Chapter 11: Settling at Mbabzi

Bruce and Doreen stayed at No.1 house, as guests, for a few weeks before moving to their new home, at No.3 house where they lived for the next 10 years. "We did briefly live at No.4 house for a few months", Doreen explains, "but we then moved to the big house next door [No.3 house] as John and Enid moved out." Doreen describes how the kitchen was separated from the rest of the house because of all the smoke that the Dover stove made, as were the toilets, which were in a separate small brick room. "I rarely visited this at night as a leopard had been known to prowl around!"

Bruce sitting on the khonde at No.4 house, 1955.

An early photo of No.3 house in the 1950s. Irene Ellis, a close friend of Doreen's, is in the garden with her children Hugh and Hilary.

Once they moved to No.3 house, Doreen had to start to get used to living in Africa. The following excerpt from a speech Doreen made to the National Council of Women summarises the major changes in her new life:

> *"It was impressed from the start that I must learn the rules of the tropics and obey them. We wore hats in the day and slept under mosquito nets at night, took prophylactics against malaria regularly, swam only in clear flowing water.... Lighting was by a generator and all the lights were out by 9:30. Of course we had extensions but as diesel was very expensive we had to be careful.... Washing was pounded with sunlight soap and rinsed with reddish-brown water, ironing was done with a heavy charcoal iron from which sparks sometime*

flew onto and made holes in our clothes. Everything had to be ironed (to avoid the chance of putzis[8] laying eggs in our clothes).... Butter came from tins, chickens came from the villages and were small, cooking was done on a Dover stove which is a wood-burning cooker – for half the year the wood was wet and the kitchen smoked out so of course one had to have servants."

Doreen quickly became responsible for the running of the large house and garden, as well as for the half a dozen servants who worked in the house and garden. The shopping trip into town occurred on a weekly basis, and Doreen frequently travelled into town to play golf. She would play tennis both at Mbabzi and at Chitedze, where the local research station was situated and where there was a small expatriate community with whom Doreen and Bruce made very good friends.

One of the things that Doreen got involved in within her first few months of living in Nyasaland was volunteering for the St. Peter's church. She and Bruce would attend the English service at St. Peter's, which took place about once a month when the Archdeacon was able to come down from Nkhota-Kota (a lakeshore town 100 miles north of Gilongue) to lead the service. It was not too long after they started attending the services at St. Peter's that Doreen went along to a vestry meeting. She was

---

8 The putzi fly is a grub like parasite; it lays its eggs in moist areas (such as damp clothes). The parasite can penetrate the skin and grow underneath the skin's surface, where it will eventually erupt through the skin in the form of a small worm.

quickly noticed by the Parish Church Council (P.C.C) as being a young person who was interested in supporting the church, and was elected to the council, where she became the chief fundraiser. Doreen recalls her early days on the committee:

> *"To my horror there was the grand total of £1 or £2 in the account... it was suggested that I organise a Bring and Buy sale, something I had never dreamed of doing in my early twenties. This was the mid-fifties and it turned out to be a very happy occasion indeed with everyone from both Services [Chichewa and English] taking part, about 25 of us I think. It was held in the old District Commissioner's house on what is now Mthunthama Drive. I think we raised about £100, a vast sum in those days."*
> (excerpt from Doreen's speech to the National Council of Women, Chalfont-St-Peters, UK, 2012)

Following the success of the Bring and Buy sale, Doreen proceeded to organise the church's first ever fete, which again was attended by congregants from both the Chichewa and the English service. "It was a wonderful occasion," Doreen says, held in the garden outside the church. There were cake stalls (Doreen was usually in charge of one; she would write to everyone on the electoral/postal list requesting them to bake a cake); needlework stalls; a white elephant stall, which was new to Lilongwe; and side stalls for the children (including a tombola and 'hoopla'). The fete was a success, and was the start of many fundraising events organised by Doreen.

The money raised went towards paying for the church's first resident priest from England, Father Leonard Constantine. Prior to this the church only had a visiting priest, Archdeacon Guy Carleton, from Nkhota-Kota. However, bad roads during the rainy season, "and the occasional herd of elephants on the road," often meant that the Archdeacon could not get down to Lilongwe to lead the service. In later years the funds also paid for a church hall, and the rectory in the church grounds.

While Doreen was heavily involved in the church, the running of the house and her busy social life, Bruce went back to working on the farm. While Bruce had been away in the UK getting married, John Foot had decided to resign as general manager of Mbabzi, as he wanted to become an MP for the Central African Federation (the Federation is described more fully in the next chapter). Bruce speculates that John might have also resigned due to the fact that he thought Bruce was returning to Nyasaland and may want to take over his role as general manager. This put Bruce in a difficult position as he had to make a decision on whether to take John's place immediately, or look for somebody older and more experienced to try and fill the gap for a few years. Bruce was only 24 years old, recently married, and only had one year's experience at Mudi. Could he really look after all these estates on his own? Luckily for Bruce, John, while waiting to become an MP, moved to live at, and run, Nyagra (the Nyasaland Agricultural Company), a large estate which was located right next to the Barron's Monjesi estate in the north of the Dowa district. John offered to continue to look after Monjesi and the other surrounding estates for the next few years until Bruce felt confident and experienced enough to run them all. In the meantime, Bruce would try to look after all the remaining estates in the west of Lilongwe district, Mbabzi and those in the Salima district, with Frank offering as much advice and support as he could.

Following this, Bruce very quickly had to learn what was happening on the various estates. His responsibilities included deciding and organising how to get between 800 to 1,000 people from their villages in the south up to Mbabzi for the grading season; getting the cash from the bank to pay for the buying of all the crops, as well as getting the cash safely to the bank from the estates; and arranging all the transport and employee related issues, amongst many other jobs.

Bruce describes how there was a great deal of travelling involved: "For example on a Monday I would visit the Mudi and Chipala estates and spend the day going round both with the supervisors/managers, taking a packed lunch with me. The next day would be spent say going round the Mbabzi fields and crops. Wednesday and Thursday would be spent travelling to more of the other estates, such as Nakondwa and Chikombe – to reach Chikombe, down by the lakeshore, I would have to park the car, wade across a river and then cycle by bike to reach it! And then Friday would be spent back at Mbabzi sorting out all the other parts of the business."

Bruce emphasises the importance of mentioning the supervisors of the various estates. "They were good hardworking people," he says. Mudi was managed by Ken Holding, who left within a year and was succeeded by Mr. C. D. Katete ("who I recruited from the research station where he was a farm manager"). Mr. Efron Nyirongo managed Chipala, Mr. Donald McCall managed Mbabzi, and a Mr. Riordan managed the two Salima estates, Nakondwa and Chikombe. On the estates in the north of Dowa, there were two expatriate managers – Jock Meldrum who lived with his wife Dorothy at Monjesi, and Martin Cameron-Dow at Mpale, where he stayed with Alice, his wife.

While Bruce managed the crop side of the estates, Marjorie continued to run the office, with the help of a book-keeper and a clerk. Luckily for Bruce the weather was kind and the prices were good, and his first full year at running Mbabzi, and the various other estates, was a success.

It was also during Bruce's first few years at Mbabzi that his sister Sheila, after completing a degree in geography at the University of Cape Town, followed by a year of secretarial work in England, also returned home to Mbabzi. For a while she too worked at the Mbabzi office, before meeting Joe Chapman, who was living and working in Lilongwe. The couple married in 1960, where they had a lovely reception on the farm. The following year Sheila's first son, Guy, was born in the Lilongwe European hospital, and two years after that, her second son, Neil, was also born there. The family of four shortly moved to England which became their new home. Sheila, who frequently visits Mbabzi, now lives just round the corner from Bruce and Doreen's UK home in Gerrards Cross.

Chapter 12: Dinner with Dr. Banda

For those of you who have lived in Malawi, or are familiar with Malawi's history, you will be able to appreciate my surprised reaction when Bruce, while discussing the Central African Federation, casually mentions how he had dined with Dr. Hastings Kamuzu Banda while they were both in London. Bruce describes how, shortly after graduating from Oxford University, there began to be commentary in the UK press about the proposed Federation. This Federation, to be enforced by the British government, was the joining of Southern Rhodesia, Northern Rhodesia and Nyasaland to become one state, as it was thought by the British government that the three countries would develop better and stronger as one unit. At that time Southern Rhodesia was internally self-governed with its own prime minister and government who were all white Southern Rhodesians, while Northern Rhodesia and Nyasaland were still being governed by the Colonial Office from London. The vast majority of the people in Northern Rhodesia and Nyasaland, the black population, were completely opposed to this federation because they thought it would be ruled entirely by the white people from Southern Rhodesia (which was economically far

79

stronger than Northern Rhodesia and Nyasaland), and would become a state of black oppression.

The press mentioned this opposition, and in particular kept referring to a 40-something year old medical doctor, from Nyasaland, practising in London, who was supposedly leading the opposition, a Dr. Hastings Banda. Bruce tells me how, as he was returning to Nyasaland shortly to begin his career, he thought it would be interesting to meet Dr. Banda. He found his address and sent him a letter, inviting him out to dinner at the English Speaking Union. Dr. Banda accepted and the two of them met. Over dinner, Dr. Banda told Bruce of his dreams of Nyasaland being independent; he wanted Nyasaland to become "the Denmark of Africa", a prosperous country based on its agriculture and the hard work of its people. This dinner marked an historic event in Bruce's life; he was probably one of the first – if not the first – people from Nyasaland to meet Dr. Banda before he returned to Nyasaland nearly ten years later. Bruce recalls that Dr. Banda never referred to their dinner, even when they met again (on several occasions) over a decade later. However, Bruce always had the impression, with references made by one or two of Dr. Banda's associates, that Dr. Banda always remembered meeting Bruce for that dinner in London. "Perhaps Dr. Banda never showed any awareness of this as he could not be seen, once in power, showing favour to someone white," Bruce speculates. "Nonetheless, having dinner with Dr. Banda is a special memory of mine, and one I will never forget."

Chapter 13: Lake Nyasa

Within the first 12 months of Doreen living in Nyasaland, Bruce took her to visit the family cottage on the shores of Lake Nyasa. Sometimes referred to as the 'calendar lake' for its dimensions (365 miles long and 52 miles wide), today Lake Nyasa is often described as 'the lake of stars', known for its unspoilt beauty and tranquility.

A.F had acquired a cottage along the lakeshore in his early days in Nyasaland. However after his death the cottage had been sold and in later years was bought by

An early postcard of Lake Nyasa.

the Costantini family. So Bruce and Doreen would stay at Frank's cottage. This is the same cottage which all the Barrons, and many friends from Malawi and visitors from the UK, have been using for the last 50 years, and continue to use to this day.

Doreen stood in front of the guesthouse at the lake, 1950s.

The cottage, which is situated along Senga bay in the Salima district, consisted of two rooms (the present dining room and the present main bedroom). Similar to the house at Mudi that Bruce had lived in a couple of years before, the lakeshore cottage was very basic; there were no glass windows or ceilings, just a tin roof; there was no electricity and no running water, only pressure lamps, and "the old bugger" paraffin fridge. The toilet, similar to the house at the Mudi estate, was in a small brick room separate from the house, consisting of nothing but a little wooden box, known as the "thunder box". The box had a bucket underneath it, and a trap door behind it. At night the watchman would open the trap door and remove the bucket – Doreen recalls how the occasional visitor got a bit of shock as every so often the watchman would remove the bucket while visitors were still sitting on the box! The kitchen was in another separate brick room with a Dover stove. There was also a small hut for the watchmen, and a separate little grass-roofed hut, with thatched reed walls and a mud floor, for visitors. A tiny path had been cleared within the bush, leading from the cottage to the lakeshore, "where it was not unusual to find snakes slithering across the path".

Today, the bay is lined with cottages, and a few bustling fishing villages; in the evenings, when the electricity is working, the whole bay is dotted with light from these cottages. Back in 1954, across the whole of Senga bay there were only three houses, all owned by expats (two of which were holiday homes, while the owner of

Bruce on the shore at Salima, wearing a head solar topee, 'sun helmet', and a red cloth to stop the sun burning the back of the neck. A.F is in the boat on the water.

the third, Mr. F. C. Smith, had a business in Salima). Doreen recalls how primitive the whole area was along the lakeshore; the entire shoreline was all bush, both in front and around the cottage, so much so that although there was less than 25m between the cottage and the water, you could not see the lake from the cottage (unlike today).

As mosquitoes were rife alongside the lakeshore, every evening those staying in the cottage would wear 'mosquito boots': boots that were made of very soft leather or felt that came up to the knees, to protect them from being bitten by the mosquitoes. Bruce and Doreen slept under mosquito nets and used mosquito 'pumps', a little tank with a long handle sticking out of it which would pump out an insecticide. It was "a laborious little contraption" which had to be continuously pumped all evening.

Because the cottage was surrounded by such dense bush, it was not unusual to come across wild animals. Monitor lizards were very popular, and "on one occasion one of our friends was having their afternoon nap when they awoke to find one directly above their head clinging to the roof timbers!" Snakes too were common. "Another time a friend visiting the cottage came running to the main house screaming, as she had found a snake hissing at the bottom of the [thunder] box just before she was about to use it!"

When Doreen's sister Violet came to visit Nyasaland – "like me she had a love for adventure", Doreen explains – she and Bruce took her to the lake. They were asleep one evening when the watchman started hammering on the back door, shouting that there was a leopard prowling close to the house. Violet started screaming in her grass shack but couldn't be heard because there was a howling wind. Eventually the watchman helped her get to the main house, where she slept in Bruce's side of the bed, with Bruce and Doreen sharing the other half of the bed (despite Violet's leopard incident, she loved her trip to Nyasaland, and upon returning home, published a summary of her stay in the Lincolnshire local paper).

A close up of the guesthouse.

Perhaps the luckiest of escapes with wild animals at the lake was that of Mr. F.C Smith. He was in the water one early evening, when a crocodile appeared and grabbed him on his bottom. Reacting very quickly, Mr. Smith twisted round and jabbed his fingers in the crocodile's eyes, which made it back away. He managed to get himself out of the water, where his wife used a bit of her own first aid kit ("which the majority of people owned at that time"), before immediately taking him to hospital (the nearest of which would have been a couple of hours drive away), where he had to have stitches. Remarkably, he managed to leave the hospital still walking. Several years later, in the 1960s, the Queen Mother paid a visit to Nyasaland, which included a trip to Salima, where she met Mr. Smith. Wanting to be polite, the Queen asked Mr. Smith, "I understand you have been taken by a crocodile and lived to tell the tale. Where did it bite you?" He coyly replied: "Underneath." Unfortunately though, Mr. Smith died prematurely and it was thought that the crocodile bite contributed to his death.

Chapter 14: Elizabeth and Edith

As Bruce, Doreen and I continue to discuss the rest of the 1950s, Bruce explains:

"1956 was particularly memorable for two reasons: firstly we were hit by cyclone Edith, which had come over the Mozambique Channel... the second was the birth of our first child, Elizabeth Jane."

The cyclone came in April. "The government were excellent in warning everyone; people were told to 'batten down the hatches', and to take every precaution against storm damage". At Mbabzi all the windows and doors were shut and reinforced as much as possible. At Nkhota-Kota there was 20 inches of rain in 24 hours, resulting in serious flooding. By the time the cyclone reached Lilongwe, it had weakened but still brought torrential rains. Sadly many Malawians lost their homes, and a lot of the crop at Mbabzi was damaged, particularly the burley tobacco, which had been hanging in the barns and was not properly covered.

After the excitement and fear of the cyclone had died down, Doreen was left to focus on the birth of her first child. Unlike today, there was then very little information to help Doreen prepare for the birth; she relied on what other young mothers in Lilongwe had told her, and the one book she was able to find – written by Grantley Dick Reid on how to relax during pregnancy and child birth – as well as visiting the doctor once a month. As the birth drew nearer, and because Bruce was away a tremendous lot, Doreen was worried about what to do when the baby was due. She confided in her closest friend in Nyasaland, Irene, who decided it would be a good idea to have a code for when Doreen was going into labour; Doreen was to ring up the research station, where Irene was based, and declare that "the fruit basket was on its way".

A few weeks later, thinking that the fruit basket's arrival was imminent, Doreen was admitted to the Lilongwe European hospital (which no longer exists), on a Saturday evening. Just when she most needed support from her husband, it was "the done thing" for all the men to get together when a wife was going into labour, and so they went and played cricket! However, having known no better, Doreen had gone to the hospital prematurely, and the baby was not born until the following Sunday evening.

Doreen recalls being very nervous giving birth in Africa. But she had grown used to being courageous because that was the only way you could be in Nyasaland or else you couldn't survive. As Doreen says: "One just had to get on with it." There was no medication to help with the pain of giving birth in those days – the only help she had was an oxygen mask, which she was soon told to stop using because she "was overdoing it". Despite this, Elizabeth Jane, named after Doreen's mother, was born on the 21st of October (Trafalgar Day), weighing 8 pounds and 4 ounces, making her "quite a heavy baby". The doctor rang Bruce the next day and complimented Doreen on how brave she had been.

By the time Doreen came out of hospital, after being there for ten days, she had lost a lot of weight. This was confirmed when someone made a comment a few days later that she looked as if she had malaria; she looked ill from being so thin and she was also sweating profusely. The only medication that was available at that time for malaria was chloroquine. Doreen was worried about the effect of taking such medication on the milk for the baby, but was told it was imperative to cure the malaria as quickly as possible, which the course of cholorquine successfully managed to do.

Shortly after Elizabeth was born, Doreen and Bruce hired their first nanny, Sarah Tungande, who was a lovely young Malawian widow. Sarah had been married to a Duncan Tungande, a very clever and ambitious young man, a fully qualified accountant, who was tragically killed in a car crash. Sarah worked for them for over 20 years, staying on long after Elizabeth, and their second child Andrew, went away to boarding school. Years later, when Sarah retired back to her home, across the border in Zambia, she would still come and visit the family once a year. The family were all very fond of Sarah, so much so that, over 20 years later, when Elizabeth had her first daughter, she named her after Sarah.

I ask Doreen if she has any interesting stories about Elizabeth's first few years. Doreen tells me of one occasion, when she was washing Liz in her bath, where she noticed a little bump on Liz's head. She gently touched the bump on her head, and out of this bump erupted a huge grub, a few inches long. Doreen was so shocked she nearly dropped the baby. Nanny Sarah informed her that it was a putzi worm. "The putzi would lay eggs on anything damp," Doreen explains. "It had obviously laid an egg in Liz's pram on the rare occasion when it wasn't covered with a net." Aside from this it is apparent that Elizabeth, and then later on Andrew, had very few, if any, unfortunate incidents as young babies to mention. "They were both looked after very well."

From a business perspective, 1956 was not a good year, and Mbabzi lost money for the first time. Bruce recalls how they had a few money-saving schemes that they used during this year. For example, when they had to buy a new 'box-body' or 'pickup', it was slightly cheaper to buy them in Blantyre rather than in Lilongwe, and so Doreen and Marjorie travelled the 200 miles, which would take up most of the day, to Blantyre in their small car to pick up the new vehicle and then drive back to Lilongwe in convoy. Another example was the purchase of moneybags full of loose change (during the buying season they would have an abundance of pennies, shillings and sixpences). The Standard Bank of South Africa, was charging a small amount per bag to cover the costs of delivering them from Blantyre. To save that little cost Marjorie would again drive to Blantyre with one of the office assistants, in order to collect the moneybags. Bruce recalls how the bank in Lilongwe strongly objected to having to count all the little coins, which made up thousands of pounds and "took them hours to do so", before depositing them, so much so that in the end the bank agreed to transport the money up from Blantyre for free.

Chapter 15: Political tension

While Doreen was adapting to her new role as a mother, and Bruce was working flat out on the estates, the political climate of Nyasaland had been growing more and more tense, as agitation against the Federation grew. Talk within Nyasaland of Dr. Banda and how he would lead the struggle against the Federation grew stronger, and pressure from the Nyasaland African Congress (NAC), the opposition to the federal government, mounted on Dr. Banda to return to Nyasaland from Britain.

It was on the 6th of July 1958 that Dr. Banda returned to Nyasaland. He landed at Chileka airport, in Blantyre, to be met by a huge crowd of Malawians who were singing and dancing. His first words as he emerged from the airplane, before he descended the steps were: "To hell with the Federation! I have come back to break the stupid Federation!" Bruce informs me how, since Dr. Banda had left Nyasaland as a young man, forty years earlier, he had almost forgotten how to speak Chinyanja, and so a lot of his first public speeches, including those famous first words he said upon arriving back in Nyasaland, were made in English. His speeches would then be interpreted by a translator, usually by Mr. J.Z.U Tembo, the President's adviser. Bruce explains how

Mr. Tembo[9] remained a close confidant of Dr. Banda throughout his political life.

Bruce and Doreen describe the period immediately following Dr. Banda's return as being unpleasant, uncertain and very tense; because they were white, local Malawians assumed they were part of the federal government, and there was a general and wide-spread anti-white feeling throughout the country. When they drove into town to do the shopping or visit the Golf Club, Malawians would shake their fists and shout "Kwacha" (Chichewa for 'dawn') at them, which was the slogan for the NAC.

While they were waiting for Dr. Banda to return to Nyasaland to lead the fight for independence, the NAC made frequent attempts to cause trouble and give the federal government a hard time by holding meetings in public, even though these had been banned unless groups had permission from the police. The police would interject these meetings and disperse the crowds. Doreen recalls one occasion where she and a friend, the wife of the chief medical officer, were playing golf at the Lilongwe Golf Club when they heard shots being fired across the river. They quickly ran back to the clubhouse; the golf club was deserted and Doreen remembers the worry of not being able to get back to the farm safely. It turned out the firing was from police who were trying to disperse an NAC "illegal meeting", the outcome of which had led to a couple of fatalities.

---

9   After Dr. Banda's death in 1997, Mr. Tembo became the head of the Malawi Congress Party, which he is still the head of today.

This all came to a head on March the 1st 1959, when the governor in Zomba, Sir Robert Armitage, declared a State of Emergency. Dr. Banda and other leading politicians from the opposition party were arrested at dawn and sent to prison in Gwelo, Southern Rhodesia. The arrests led to unrest throughout the country, particularly up in the Northern region, including on the Barron's estates in the north of the Dowa district. A few days later Doreen and Bruce got a nasty shock when three European families who were managing the three estates – the Coles, Mickey Turner and his girlfriend, and the Clenches – appeared at No.3 house as they had been chased off the estates. They were all very frightened and in a state of shock, having been threatened by NAC supporters. Bruce and Doreen took them in and they stayed at Mbabzi for a couple of weeks until things had quieted down.

To try and maintain the peace, as well as reassure the safety of the expat community, the 'Special Constables' were formed, a small volunteer group of about 20 men, of all ages and sizes, including Bruce, the Costantini men and Bruce and Doreen's close friend Rex. "There was a humorous element to it," Doreen explains, "It all reminded me a bit of Dad's Army!" Every evening they would meet on the old airfield[10] (by the present Mchinji roundabout where Area 9 is currently situated), where they practised a bit of drill. They would then patrol around the area, watching out for people attempting to cause trouble. On one occasion Bruce was on patrol

---

10 This had been recently closed down, and a new airport had been opened, situated halfway between Mbabzi and Lilongwe. Today this new airport is the army airwing and headquarters.

with a friend, when they saw a man in a suit walking briskly with a briefcase. Thinking he may be a politician with important information, they confronted him and asked to search his briefcase. The man bashfully opened his briefcase and revealed its contents to them – it was empty except for a couple of sandwiches!

While Bruce and his friends were involved in being Special Constables, the colonial governor in Zomba took more serious action and called on the federal government, based in Southern Rhodesia, to send in soldiers (who were to be somewhat more effective than the Special Constables!), to help restore law and order. Bruce and Doreen have a strong recollection of the soldiers – who were not part of the regular troops, but members of the general public who had been called up to assist – being flown in from Salisbury. They were camping at the airport, three miles from Mbabzi Estate. Despite being a scary time, the arrival of the army provided some additional company for Bruce and Doreen; Doreen and her friends formed a canteen for them at the airport – they would bake cakes at home which they would then hand out to the soldiers. Bruce and Doreen also happened to know one of the soldiers and invited them all round to dinner several times at No.3 house. The soldiers all stomped into the house, placing their guns in a corner. Bruce laughs as he recalls how, upon entering the living room, the chief officer exclaimed, "A fat lot of use those guns are up against the corner!"

Unfortunately the army were not well received by the general public, and there was an increase in the number of breakouts as Malawians retaliated against them. Numerous incidents of people being shot or wounded occurred throughout the country. "This included a Colonial government officer who happened to be visiting one of our estates, who was attacked,' says Bruce. "He was luckily rescued and escaped with a broken leg – it could have been a lot worse."

The worst incident, which has since become historical, occurred on March the 3rd 1959 at Nkhata Bay, a lakeshore village in the north of the country. An illegal meeting was taking place which the army tried to disperse, firing into the crowd after warnings. There was a lot of bloodshed and a total of 19 people were killed[11]. Bruce describes how it was such a horror and shock hearing about what had happened, and how it led to an increased feeling of fear as people were worried about the repercussions. The following is an excerpt from a letter sent by Mr. R.A Leach, who was working for the Colonial Development Corporation in South Kasungu, to Bruce three days after March the 3rd, highlighting the trouble caused on one of the estates:

---

11 Since then, the 3rd of March is remembered as Martyrs Day and is a public holiday in Malawi.

> **Colonial Development Corporation**   Memorandum
>
> From: R. A. Leach
> To: B. Barron Esq., Mbabzi Estate
> Date: 6th March, 1959
>
> Dear Bruce,
>
> I am sending this letter by hand of Nigel Coles to you, a copy of which George Foot has taken for Vic Milward if you think necessary.
>
> As they will all tell you a very dangerous situation developed on Wednesday in the Mponela / Madisi / Nyagra area during which parties of Africans ran wild, and Colin Bundy was seriously injured. Nigel Coles mercifully gave the alarm and I was able to get help from Michael Harris at Kasungu, who sent Police and Troops. Situation in the area has since been quiet after the clearing of numerous road blocks and the arrests of several people. There is ample evidence that it will not remain so for long and the situation will become critical if anything happens, as our troops at Kasungu have been moved back to Lilongwe this morning.
>
> We will not be able in these circumstances to give any great help to your people, the Foots and the Belks should anything further occur after they go back. At present it would be unwise without military protection in the immediate area.
>
> Decisions must be made by the authorities as to what they are going to do, and what is to happen to the Belks who are completely cut off from help if anything happens.
>
> Everybody is welcome to stay here as long as they like, but I feel the authorities must make arrangements for billeting etc. and the security of estates.
>
> They will be reporting on the inadequacy of security arrangements and lack of a pre-arranged plan. Michael Harris has taken all the brunt of this trouble when it has not been his responsibility and behaved and co-operated extremely well. His request for air observation on Mpali before the Coles were got out was never answered, in fact we have not seen a spotting plane for over a week. A flight over the estates daily to spot the letter "T" has only been done once, ten days ago !!
>
> I hope this will enable you to make the very strongest representations to the authorities.
>
> Yours sincerely,
>
> Richard Leach

Although the 3rd of March was by far the worst incident that occurred, tensions and disturbances continued, as evidenced by the letter below. Written by Mr. G. "Mickey" Turner (manager of Nkonde estate), this was sent to Bruce nearly a month after the state of emergency, summarising the occurrences at Nkonde:

> Nkonde Estate,
> 2nd April 1959.
>
> ### Report on the lack of adequate Security Patrols on Nkonde Estate from 3rd - 31st March
>
> The undermentioned will show when the estate was visited, the dates, and by whom, contrary to pre-arranged plans at meetings of the Security Forces.
>
> **3rd March.** Three Africans on bicycles pulled down barriers around the Manager's house at 3.30 p.m. whilst the Manager was away from estate. On his return a guard was placed on the house but Africans continued to prowl around all night.
>
> **4th March.** 5.30 a.m. A mob started assembling through the estate making a special point of causing a nuisance and parading around the house.
>
> 6.30 a.m. Capitao advised manager to leave the estate. 7 a.m. Manager left for Mpali estate. (and was only too glad to)
>
> The road through the estate along to Monjesi was constantly paraded by Africans who were trying to intimidate the Capitao and tenants. The capitao and family finally left their house.
>
> **5th March.** Returned to estate with Army patrol. Plenty of intimidation at night.
>
> **6th March.** As above
>
> **8th March.** Visited estate again with two other managers from Mbabzi Estates.
>
> **9th March.** Visited estate again as above.
>
> **16th March.** Visited the estate by myself and stayed for the day.
>
> **17th March.** Visited the estate with the Mbabzi Manager. C.D.C. Patrol.
>
> **18th March.** Moved permanently back to the estate, replaced the barriers. Barriers were removed during the night. Names were taken.
>
> **19th March.** Went on patrol with N. Coles around the neighbouring estates. The agreement then was that my estate should be visited every three days.
>
> 22nd March. No patrol.

Slowly, over the next few months it all eventually quieted down, and by the following year, 1960, the country was relatively stable and peaceful. The government in the UK and the colonial secretary insisted that Dr. Banda be released, after a year of being imprisoned, and talks soon began with him and the NAC with a view to having elections. It was also at this time that Doreen discovered she was pregnant again; this brought excitement and happiness, a nice change from the fear and stress that had prevailed during the State of Emergency.

Nine months later, on Monday the 2nd of November 1959, Andrew Graeme ("we nearly called him Murray after one of Bruce's uncles") was born, weighing 8 pounds 9 ounces. It was a long labour, all day Sunday and Monday until 9:00pm, ending in a rather difficult birth, which was helped along by nurse Tommy Jeffery. A few years later Nurse Jeffrey came to live at No.4 house with her husband, where they lived for around 30 years. Her husband had lost his job in Lilongwe and so Bruce and Doreen offered them No.4 house to stay in, rent free, while he searched for another job. She became a close and loyal friend of the Barrons for many years, and, over 25 years later, was there to help with the first few weeks of Andrew's wife Sheila's first-born daughter.

In terms of tobacco production, 1958 started as a big worry: for the first time since Bruce had been managing Mbabzi the rains failed in March. Luckily it all turned out well and the Barrons had a big crop – probably selling over 2/3rds of the country's burley. The following year, because all of the deliberate damage that had been done with the riots and outbreaks, the company made a loss.

Chapter 16: Independence

The 1960s brought huge change to Nyasaland. The first elections took place in 1961; Dr. Banda and his party won every seat. He was consequently asked by the governor, on advice from the colonial secretary, to become prime minister and take charge of Nyasaland's internal affairs within the federation, working under Glyn Jones. The federation formally came to an end in 1963, and Northern Rhodesia, Southern Rhodesia, and Nyasaland became semi-independent countries. The following year Nyasaland became a fully independent country, and two years later in 1966, Dr. Banda became the country's first President.

For Bruce and Doreen, the 1960s were a period of immense stress and anxiety, which first started when Bruce, wondering if Dr. Banda would remember their meeting in London nearly 10 years ago, invited Dr. Banda to visit Mbabzi to show him how the estates were being run. This was in 1961[12]; Dr. Banda had been released from prison and appointed as Minister of Agriculture by the Governor.

---

12   It was at this time that the governor of Nyasaland, Robert Armitage, retired, and was succeeded by Sir Glynn Jones (who was previously the Chief Secretary in Zambia).

'I invited him to visit Mbabzi and see the Central Region tenant farming system on the ground. He accepted but it all went wrong. It turned into a huge political rally with a lot of strong language and [subsequently there were a lot of] veiled threats about the estates.' (notes from a speech made by Bruce Barron, 1990s)

Hundreds of tenants and labourers had gathered to see Dr. Banda upon his visit to Mbabzi Dr. Banda took advantage of this by trying to gain further support for the fight against the federation. Bruce describes how he would start all his speeches by punching his fist into the air, shouting the freedom mantra: "Kwacha, kwacha!", followed by "Ufuru, ufuru!" (freedom), and then "Ntendere, ntendere!" (peace). He would shout these words in a passionate and aggressive manner to stir up the crowds and get their attention.

Following this visit, Dr. Banda made a strong public attack on the estates, specifically on the tenant system. He referred to it as a bad system, comparable to that of the sharecropping system in America. Dr. Banda then made a statement to all estate owners, declaring that they had exactly one year to give up the system and revert to the 'normal' means of growing crops with paid labourers. This came as a big shock and it was extremely worrying for all those at Mbabzi.

For the first year following Dr. Banda's demand, Bruce made the decision not to make any changes to the farming system at Mbabzi; it was simply too difficult and uneconomical, and so he decided to carry on with things the way they were and see what happened. This didn't go unnoticed and after one year of being warned, Dr. Banda issued another stronger warning. Despite the serious risk of having his land taken away from him, or possibly even being deported (once independence, which was seemingly imminent, was granted) from Nyasaland, Bruce still continued to make no changes to the tenant system. Although not yet the President, Dr. Banda was the senior politician and head of the National Congress Party; it is therefore a great understatement to say it was rather bold of Bruce not to have made any changes. As yet another year passed, and the situation got increasingly risky, Bruce put a back-up plan in place: he sent one of the Mbabzi managers, Nigel Coles, down to Southern Rhodesia to see if there was any farm land available that they may be able to move to, should they suddenly be forced to leave.

Amongst all the political change happening during this time, Bruce and Doreen talk of a more light-hearted moment when Sir Roy Welensky, the prime minister of the federation, came to visit Nyasaland to support the United Federal Party, the political party in opposition to Dr. Banda and the NAC. He stayed with them at Mbabzi at No.3, bringing with him an entourage of heavy security who stayed in the neighbouring No.4 house. It was during one evening that Bruce and Doreen started hearing shouts from outside, sounding like someone was yelling "Banda! Banda!" They had already been a little nervous about how Malawians would react when they found out Welensky was staying with them, and so assumed it was Dr. Banda supporters who were coming to protest against, or possibly attack, Welensky. Within moments the security team barged into Bruce and Doreen's house, locked Welensky in the guest bedroom, and went outside to face the protesters. Instead they found Gordon[13] and Freida Dougal, who lived at No.5 house searching amongst the bushes; they had lost their little terrier, called Panda, and were out looking for her! The security team quickly went back inside and unlocked Welensky from his bedroom.

Following Malawi's independence, members of the cabinet became increasingly frustrated with Dr. Banda and wanted to revolt at the slow progress of localisation. They wanted a new government in place, one which removed the many white civil servants, and if necessary, Dr. Banda as well. A cabinet crisis ensued. But with help from political allies plus support from the army and police, Dr. Banda was able to quell the revolt, and the leaders of the revolt fled. One of the leaders, Kanyama Chiume, moved to Tanzania, while another, Masauko Chipembere, went back to his home district along the southern lakeshore before secretly leaving the country in 1965[14].

This major challenge to Dr. Banda's authority put the "troublesome" estates very much on the backburner – he issued them with another warning, announcing they

---

13 Gordon moved to Mbabzi in 1956 to replace Tommy Parkinson in being responsible for all of Mbabzi's transport.

14 Chipembere lived the rest of his life in exile, most of it in California, after his attempts a few years later to reconcile with Banda and be allowed back into the country came to nothing. Chiume was given permission to return in 1994. He lived most of the rest of his life in Malawi, before dying in New York in 2007.

now had five years in which to change their system. For the time being, little attention was given to the estates and Bruce was able to continue producing tobacco (which was now all burley) peacefully. As Doreen says, "it was Nyasaland's independence that saved us from potentially losing everything!"

Although politically and from a business point of view these years were fraught for Bruce and Doreen, from a personal side it was an exciting time for their two children, as Liz and Andrew both started their schooling (Liz in 1961, and Andrew in 1964) at the Lilongwe European School. The school's name was later changed to Bishop Mackenzie School, named after Charles Mackenzie, one of the very early Christian missionaries in Nyasaland (the school still exists today, and is where Andrew's three children, including myself, had their primary education). Bruce soon joined the schools Parents and Teachers Association (PTA), where he was involved in many fundraising events.

However, as the federation came to an end and many of the federation employees based in Nyasaland returned to Southern Rhodesia, the number of pupils started to dwindle. Doreen recalls a Mrs. Marks, one of Liz's teachers, informing Bruce and Doreen that Liz "had a good brain" and that she ought to be sent elsewhere since there was not enough competition for her in Lilongwe. And so Doreen and Bruce made the decision to enroll Liz at Bishopslea School in Salisbury (now Harare), as a full time boarder aged just eight. A few years later, as numbers continued to decrease at Bishop Mackenzie, from 200 pupils to just 60, Andrew too was sent to boarding school in Rhodesia. Doreen recalls the first time arriving back "to the huge wretch of the empty house", having waved off both their children to boarding school at a very early age for the very first time.

Andrew, aged eight, alongside Dina, on the first day of being sent to boarding school in Rhodesia, 1968.

Chapter 17: Losing land and friends

The late 1960s presented Bruce with an opportunity to take his mind off the worry over the estates; the Capital City Development Cooperation (the CCDC) was setup by the President, and Bruce received a letter appointing him on the Board of directors. The aim of the CCDC was to move the capital city from Zomba to Lilongwe. "This was a very good decision as it was intended to spread development more evenly throughout the country," Bruce remarks. Prior to the move, economic and government activity had been heavily concentrated in the south; all the government ministries, embassies, and commercial head offices (e.g. for the tobacco industry, motor industry, retail etc.) were based in the south.

Bruce recalls the excitement of the planning group as they stood in the little viewing tower which had been built in the middle of what is now City Centre. They surveyed the surrounding land, which at the time was complete bush. The land was to be divided into three areas; one for housing (Bruce recalls the present Area 12 being the first housing area to be built), one for commercial businesses, and one for industrial use. The excitement continued as the work started and the shape of the landscape began to change. The initial work was financed by apartheid South Africa – which Banda was the only African leader to establish ties with – who issued a grant of 5 million rand.

The first ministry, the Ministry of Works, was opened a few years later, and others soon followed. Then the embassies began their move, starting with South Africa, followed by the UK, whose new high commission was opened by Owen Griffith, the deputy high commissioner. Bruce and Doreen became very close friends with his whole family (and are still friendly to this day).

In addition to the CCDC, the World Bank sponsored a new initiative, the Lilongwe Land Development Scheme, the aim of which was to revitalise the agricultural industry in Lilongwe. The move of all the embassies and major businesses from Zomba to Lilongwe, as well as the World Bank scheme, transformed Bruce and Doreen's social lives as more and more people moved from the southern region to live in the new commercial hub of Lilongwe. They made lots of new friends and greatly enjoyed the expansion of their previously very small community.

However, just as things were starting to look more positive for Bruce and Doreen – pressure from the government over their estates had eased, and Lilongwe was buzzing with new developments and lots of new faces – things took a turn for the worse and Bruce and Doreen hit a new low point.

It was in 1969 when Bruce received a communication requesting him to meet Bryan Roberts, the Secretary to the President and Cabinet. Bryan informed Bruce that the President felt that he had too many estates, to which Bruce rather boldly said that was correct. He then asked Bruce if he would give up any of his estates. This was a huge and sudden shock to Bruce. After a few moments of silence Bruce agreed, and offered to give up the three blocks of adjoining land in Kasungu, and the estate which was on the Bua river in the Lilongwe river – a total of 3,000 acres. Bryan declared that "this would go down very well."

The following week a rally was held at the Kasungu estate at which Dr. Banda attended to officially announce the handover. Thousands of Malawians gathered to see Dr. Banda. Bruce too attended but tried to remain out of sight, at the back of all the crowds. Bruce recalls the President saying to the crowds that it was not because the estates were badly run that they were being taken away from Mr. Barron, but because it was "time for a change". He then addressed Bruce, simply announcing that "Mr. Barron is not a bad man". He also declared how the estates would continue to be run the same way as they had been before, although there was no mention of the tenant system. A complete u-turn; instead of banning the tenant system as he had been trying to get the Barrons to do for the last several years, Dr. Banda joined it! The Kasungu estate was given to Press Agricultural Ltd., a presidential holding group, and the Bua estate was given to Mama Cecilia Tamanda Kadzamira, Banda's official hostess.

Glad that the handover had gone relatively smoothly, and thinking that that this was the end of it, Bruce returned back to running the rest of Mbabzi and the other estates, trying not to dwell on the fact that he had just lost four of his estates. However, Bruce was soon summoned again, this time to meet the President himself, in Zomba. Accompanying the President was a senior politician, the secretary general of the Malawi Congress Party.

Banda produced a hand-drawn map which had lots of blobs scattered across the map which were one of three colours – red, green or blue. Looking more closely, Bruce realised that the areas in red marked the Conforzi estates, the green areas were the Wallace estates and the blue areas covered the Barrons land. The President tapped one of the larger blue blobs, declaring that he wanted the Barrons estates in Madisi, as he still thought Bruce had too much. These consisted of Mpale, Monjesi, Nkonde and Nyagra (the latter, which was run by John Foot for a few years, was taken over by the Barrons when John Foot was offered a cabinet post and had to move to Salibury (Harare)) – totalling between 7,000 and 8,000 acres. Taking a deep breath he replied, "Your Excellency, may we please keep the Madisi estates and you take the big estates in the Mudi river area." A long silence followed. In that silence, Bruce didn't know whether he was going to be taken out of the country on the next plane or shot at dawn – challenging the President in his request was an incredibly risky thing to do. Eventually the President burst out laughing and said, "All right Mr. Barron, you can keep the Madisi estates and I will have those others". He then turned to his officials and said, "Mudi Estate will go to Chamwavi [a group of his personal estates] and the other estate, Chipala, to Press Agricultural Ltd." That was the end of the meeting and Bruce was dismissed.

This meant that by the end of the 1971 season Bruce was left with the four estates in Madisi, one at Salima and Mbabzi. Bruce was not the only estate owner who was asked to give up his land; both Simon Wallace and the Conforzis lost all their estates in the central region (with the exception of Lingadzi for the Wallaces); fortunately they were both able to keep their land in the southern region.

Bruce was subsequently informed that they would be paid nothing for the land which they were giving up, but they would be paid the valuations of the improvements (e.g. roads or buildings which had been built on the estates). A few years later, when Bruce started to query some of the valuations, he was quietly told by a government official to shut up and that he should be grateful he was to get anything at all. In the end he was paid out over 10 years at 3% of the valuation.

What the Barrons had left was still viable, but Bruce did have to lay off two expatriate managers, Andrew Tullach and Sam Sylvester. Andrew had been living at No.2 house and was responsible for running the group of estates that the President had taken away from Bruce (Chipala, Mudi and Kasanjola), while Sam, who had been living at No.6 house, was working as a manager at Mbabzi.

Once again Bruce hoped this would be the last of it and once again turned his attention to running the remaining estates. Three years later and Bruce was asked to see the new Secretary to the President and Cabinet, George Jaffu, who had taken over from Bryan Roberts at the Lilongwe Hotel. George delivered a message from the

President saying that he wanted more estates. Bruce's heart sank, but he had no choice other than to agree. And so the Mpale and Nkonde estates from Madisi, which he had tried so hard to keep hold of, and Nakondwa from Salima, were all handed over to the government, totaling another 4,000 acres. Once again Bruce was promised that would be the last of it. This left the Barrons with Nyagra and Monjesi in the Madisi area and the home farm of Mbabzi – two out of the original 16 (Nyagra was bought at a later date).

The unpleasantness continued. Towards the end of 1974, some close friends, Tony and Elizabeth Millership, were declared PI's (Prohibited Immigrants), for having been overheard making mild criticism of the government. They had to leave the country immediately and Doreen had the sad task of packing up their house. "Wash baskets, photo frames, the dogs baskets, everything had to go – oh, it was awful!" Doreen explains. All the family possessions were sent to No.1 house, transported in Bruce and Doreen's cars, an Mbabzi lorry and box-body, and kept in the billiard room.

Very soon after that, another one of Bruce and Doreen's friends, the Anglican vicar at St. Peter's Church, the Reverend Jack Biggers, was also declared a P.I[15]. He too was a good friend. "I remember taking him to the airport to say goodbye, which was very sad," Bruce remarks. Once again Doreen had to help pack up the house.

---

15 Fortunately, Rev. Jack Biggers returned to Malawi 20 years later as the first Anglican Bishop of the new Diocese of Northern Malawi.

"Following this there was an even bigger blow," Bruce continues. The general manager of Mbabzi, Nigel Coles, who had worked there for 19 years, and whose family had become very close friends with the Barrons, "had an incident" at the Mpale estates.

Nigel had made the decision to sack the Malawian supervisor at Mpale. However the supervisor was a popular man in the local village, and there was a big backlash against Nigel's decision, with many unhappy and annoyed tenants. Bruce thought it was best to keep the peace amongst the employees, and advised Nigel to reinstate the supervisor and instead give him an official warning. Nigel agreed with Bruce's decision. A meeting was held where Nigel announced this to the tenants, who all clapped and cheered at the news. At the end of the meeting Nigel asked if there were any other questions. One of the tenants stood up and asked Mr. Coles why he had made a critical remark about the President on a previous occasion. Unfortunately for Nigel the local police, who were also friends of the supervisor, had attended the meeting, and were obliged to send a report to Zomba about Nigel's 'critical' comments regarding the President.

It was a couple of months later, after painfully waiting to hear the outcome of the report, that a police Land Rover drove up the No.1 house driveway. A very senior police officer emerged from the car. He had been sent there by the inspector general to serve Mr. Coles with a notice declaring him a Prohibited Immigrant. Bruce and Doreen were devastated. Bruce informed the officer that Nigel was in Salisbury, Southern Rhodesia. The officer then instructed Bruce to call him and ask him to return to Malawi immediately, but not to say nothing about the deportation order, so that it could be served on him personally when he returned, "a horrible thing to do," Bruce remarks. As soon as the officer left, Bruce headed straight into town to meet the acting deputy British high commissioner to see if anything could be done to help Nigel, but had no luck. As a last resort he then drove to Blantyre to see Cyril Marowe, the chief immigration officer, whom Bruce and Doreen knew well. Cyril said he had already been informed about the situation, and that his officers in Salisbury had notified the Coles that they were Prohibited Immigrants and could therefore not return to their home. There was nothing more that Bruce could do. So once again Doreen had to pack up another house. But this was a family with whom Bruce and Doreen's children had grown up with. "The whole thing was very traumatic," Doreen explains. Not only did they have to deal with the loss of a family who was very close to them and their children, there was the constant worry in the back of their minds about whether they might be next to go.

As a result of the Coles deportation, Brian Piers who had joined the company in 1972, and had been managing Mbabzi, was promoted to general manager of all the estates to replace Nigel Coles, in 1975. Brian and his wife Stephanie stayed happily at Mbabzi for 11 years before leaving to go to Australia. Bruce remarks how Brian was "a huge assistance in helping to run the estates; he and I made a very good combination working together." The Piers were then succeeded by Peter Buttress and his wife Mary-Ann.

After the trauma of three deportations, especially that of the Coles with their 20 year association with the Barrons, Bruce and Doreen had to be very careful with how they behaved, dressed and what they said. In terms of clothing, Dr. Banda had banned ladies from wearing mini-skirts or trousers (with the exception of traditional Asian clothes), while men were not allowed to have long hair. Bruce and Doreen were constantly aware that one step out of line and they could be thrown out of the country. They considered themselves very much at risk which was a long, never-ending worry. "Bruce became ill with strain," says Doreen. It was not until a few years later that the political situation eased and Bruce and Doreen felt less exposed, and could relax a little bit.

There was one final, somewhat awkward, incident involving Simon Wallace and Bruce around the same time. They had both been asked if they could build bigger schools on their Lilongwe estates for the local children in the villages to attend, which they agreed to. This greatly pleased the then education minister, Rodwell Munyenyembe.

The two schools that they built, Lingadzi secondary school and Mbabzi primary school, still exist today and provide education to the children of the tenants, labourers and other employees working on the estates, as well as to children in the surrounding villages. At the beginning of this academic year, 2,098 children were enrolled at Mbabzi school – with only 26 teachers; over 85 children per class! Over the last decade the school has had support from both Bruce and myself. To celebrate Bruce's 80th birthday Bruce started a library at the school. At the time it consisted of a small room with a dozen or so donated books. The library has steadily grown over the years and now has over 10,000 books spread across four rooms complete with electricity, desks and chairs. It is a huge asset not only to the children at the school but to the entire community. Meanwhile I set up a charity to support the schools, the Mbabzi Schools Project, which, amongst other projects, has funded desks for all the classes and four new classrooms.

After building the two schools on their respective estates, Bruce and Simon were summoned to see the minister of health in her Blantyre office. Once they had entered her office, the minister said she knew they had small clinics on the estates but now wanted a hospital built. Bruce started to ask a few questions about who would run it and who would provide the drugs when he was abruptly interrupted and told to do it or their estates would be expropriated.

She then called in two medical officers and told them that these two men have offered to build a hospital and could they be shown the plans of the Blantyre district hospital. She informed Bruce and Simon that she would be sending officers from her ministry to check on the progress of the work.

Not being left much choice, Bruce and Simon started making plans with the officials, which Bruce adds was much more productive and easygoing than with the minister of health. Soon after that the minister lost her position as she was connected with the late Albert Muwalo, the secretary general of the MCP (who allegedly attempted a coup against Banda and was later hanged). It was subsequently agreed with the health ministry that the hospital was not needed, but that a greatly expanded clinic would be sufficient. Soon after the clinic was expanded, Bruce and Simon shared the costs of the building and the government continued, and to this day continues, to provide and pay for the staff and drugs.

Chapter 18: The shipwreck

One of most exciting stories that Bruce and Doreen have told me about has to be when they were aboard the Ilala, the largest passenger carrying boat on the lake.

In 1977 Bruce and Doreen, with a group of four friends, went aboard the ship for a seven day cruise up and down the lake. "The ship was wonderful," Doreen explains. "It had a huge open deck with a half a dozen or so first class double cabins and space for several hundred lower deck passengers."

They boarded the ship at Chipoka (near Salima) and sailed northwards to Nkhota-Kota[16], where they docked for the night. The next day the Ilala sailed across the lake to the islands of Likoma[17] and Chisamulu[18]. At each

---

16 At the time Nkhota-Kota was one of the largest villages in Central Africa, and formerly a very large staging centre for the slave trade. Slaves were put on Arab dhows and taken across the lake en route to Zanzibar or even further afield to the Middle East.

17 On Likoma island is the very large Anglican cathedral modelled on Winchester cathedral. Made of burnt brick, it was constructed at the beginning of the 20th century. Likoma was also the headquarters of the U.M.C.A (the University's Mission to Central Africa).

18 Chisamulu is a very small island a few miles west of Likoma inhabited by a few villages.

The MV Ilala (taken from kot-w-kaloszach.blogspot).

stop the ship would lower its two 3-ton steel lifeboats which took the passengers to and from the shores. They then continued their journey across the lake to Nkhata Bay, the then main port for the northern region. From here the Ilala sailed slowly northwards along the lake shoreline, calling at remote settlements nestled at the foot of the lakeshore mountains. At each of these settlements passengers in the 2nd and 3rd classes would embark and disembark, dropping off supplies – ranging from maize and furniture to chickens – to their home villages. "In the case of Likoma island, a lot of them dropped off firewood," says Doreen, who wrote about the trip in her journal, in 1977. In it is written how the Ilala was like *"a lifeline to these remote places"*. She also notes how *"the whole scenery was reminiscent of a Scottish loch or a Norwegian fjord rather than a tropical lake."*

They sailed onwards to Chilumba, and then Karonga. Upon arriving at Karonga, Doreen describes how a crowd of Malawians quickly formed, the majority of whom had probably never seen white people before, let alone a group of them. Several ran away as the group walked along the beach.

Doreen wrote in her journal, *'Karonga itself was fascinating because of its history.'* It had been the centre of the slave trade in the area and the focal point for attacks by the antislavery forces, such as the the African Lakes Corporation and the colonial government, against traders. Also at Karonga is a beautifully maintained cemetery dating from one of the very first engagements of W.W.I, on the 8th September 1914, when British and German troops clashed a few miles inland (Germany occupied German East Africa, which included parts of today's Burundi, Rwanda and Tanzania). The soldiers lie buried side by side – there are two lines of officers, one of Germans and one of the English, with a memorial table to the *Askari* (African soldiers who fought as part of the King's African Rifles) at the entrance of the cemetery. "Since then the lake level has risen," Bruce explains, "and they've had to move all the graves further back."

It was during the journey back down the lake, where they called in at the same places in the reverse order, that the weather started to turn a little unpleasant. It is written in Doreen's journal how *"all week there had been normal lake shore storms blowing up in the evenings, and early mornings, typical of the rainy season."* Early the following morning, *"it was on a Wednesday"*, at around 5am, Doreen, half-asleep, was woken by a huge bang. They heard the engine stop and the banging continued. There was a knock at the door and a first officer appeared, instructing them to put their life jackets on and go up to the deck immediately. They did as instructed and staggered up to the top deck. Within seconds they were drenched to the skin. The deck was empty; Bruce looked in to the bridge where the captain quickly said they were in the wrong place – "it is far too dangerous to be up here!" – and ordered them to go down to the saloon. Once down in the saloon Bruce recalls meeting another family who were also staying in 1st class, a Malawian doctor and his wife escorting their grandson down to Blantyre.

Bruce and Doreen soon realised that the ship had been pushed towards an outcrop of rocks, banging into one which created a huge hole just below their cabin. "It was badly flooded but the crew managed to seal the hole off with several mattresses," says Doreen. A message came from the captain, telling everyone to quickly go back to their cabin, and choose one of their possessions to take with them. Doreen chose her bag of medicine, while Bruce joked how he wanted to take a razor so he could shave. "What did other people take with them?" I ask. Bruce and Doreen listed some of items they remember seeing: a bible, two bottles of wine, and rather bizarrely, a bunch of long grasses that someone had picked up from Karonga.

Because the wind was so strong, the lifeboats couldn't be used – the one lifeboat that they had lowered down to the water as a test quickly got overturned by the wind and smashed against the rock. As a result, some of the 2nd and 3rd class passengers, out which there were over 300, had started jumping overboard, some not even waiting to get hold of lifejackets, hoping to be able to swim to shore. One woman who jumped hit a rock where she broke an arm and consequently died of shock. Miraculously, this was the only life that was lost.

Eventually the wind died down, but by this point the Ilala was well and truly wedged onto the rock. As mid-morning approached they received another announcement from the chief steward, who declared that breakfast was now ready. As if nothing had happened, he then apologised that the grapefruit juice was not chilled and that he hoped fried eggs and baked beans was acceptable. While breakfast was being served, the captain sent a message to the President who alerted a ship from the southern end of the lake, at Monkey Bay, to go and rescue the passengers.

After a long morning of sitting in the sun and waiting, "where I fell asleep and got terribly sunburnt," says Doreen, a breeze suddenly picked up from the other direction and blew the Ilala off the rock. Slowly, the crew were gradually able to skim the ship over the rocky base until they reached deep water where they anchored. "Shortly after this the Mpasa – a ship that happened to be within the area and was sent to assess the Ilala's damage – turned up," Doreen explains. On board the ship included the minister of transport and communications and the chairman and the general manager of the railways. Rather remarkably there was also an Icelandic diver, *"the only professional diver in Malawi at the time"* – aboard the ship, and Rod Capper, another diver and friend of Bruce and Doreen. He, and the others, had flown to Likoma island and happened to be on an afternoon cruise when they received a message from the President's office. Mr. Kappa inspected the damage and informed the passengers that a tugboat from Monkey Bay would arrive the following morning to rescue them. So Bruce, Doreen and all the other passengers had to endure another night on the Ilala, which was terribly worrying; the ship's hole had only been temporarily repaired and there was the possibility of another strong wind starting up again.

Luckily the night was quiet and non-eventful, and the following morning, as promised, the tug arrived, picking up all the passengers and taking them back to shore at Nkhata Bay. When they docked at Nkhata Bay, they could hear large crowds singing somber hymns and songs. As the passengers approached, they were looked at with some animosity and dislike from the crowds, with lots of murmuring about them as they walked from the dock to the vehicles that were waiting to take them back to Lilongwe. Nothing to do with the shipwreck, the crowd had gathered because it was March the 3rd, Martyrs Day in Malawi, where those who died during the uprising in 1959 were remembered – not an ideal day for a group of people, the majority of whom were expats, to be taken there!

Bruce and Doreen travelled by Land Rover and lorry to Mzuzu where they boarded a plane to take them back to Lilongwe. It was at breakfast the next day when they learned that during the last night aboard the shipwrecked Ilala the captain had not slept at all – they were only half a mile away from the Mozambican coast where missiles were being prepared for the civil war there and were frequently being used in that area of water! A fact which he had wisely kept to himself.

The Ilala was soon properly repaired and today still transports Malawians living along the lakeshore up and down the lake.

Chapter 19: The Queen, Margaret Thatcher and other VIP visitors

Every now and then during our interview sessions, Bruce and Doreen will mention some of the VIP dinners and events they were invited to, and some of the famous people they have met.

One of the most exciting occasions undoubtedly has to be meeting Queen Elizabeth, the Queen Mother, in 1960[19]. What was equally as exciting to find out was that the Queen Mother was scheduled to visit Mbabzi. Well, a slight exaggeration, perhaps, as the trip to Mbabzi was a back-up plan in case she was unable to fly to Mzuzu (where she was scheduled to be staying, at the provincial commissioner's house), due to bad weather. But for the weeks leading up to her visit Bruce and Doreen knew that there was a chance that the Queen Mother may come to Mbabzi. An incredible honour and huge privilege, Bruce made every effort to make sure Mbabzi was 'Queen appropriate' – trees were trimmed, lawns were mowed and houses were cleaned. Smart white rope

---

19 This was the Queen Mother's second visit to Malawi; the first was pre-Independence.

was put up around the bwalo and the house staff were bought brand new smart white uniforms with matching gloves. Disappointingly, the Queen Mother never got to see any of this as the weather was clear on the day and so she was able to fly up to Mzuzu instead. A group of VIPs were sent up to Mzuzu to meet and greet her, among them were Frank and Marjorie.

Back at Mbabzi, the disappointment of the Queen Mother not visiting did not last long, as Bruce and Doreen were then asked if some of her staff and retinue could come to No.3 house for lunch, as the plane to Mzuzu was a small one and could only seat a few people. The entourage included the Queen's hairdresser, the BBC royal correspondent (Audrey Russell) and a few other BBC correspondents. Bruce recalls how extremely interesting it was being able to meet these people and hear the inside details of accompanying a royal visit.

Just under 20 years later the Queen returned to Nyasaland as part of her Commonwealth tour, and Bruce and Doreen were invited to Sanjika Palace, the President's residence in Blantyre, for a reception and state dinner in honour of the Queen. "Oh it was so exciting," Doreen explains, "all the ladies bought special evening dresses from England for the occasion." She continues to describe how the road up to Sanjika Palace, which is situated on top of a big hill, was lined with hundreds of lights all the way up to the top. "It really looked like something out of a fairytale." Bruce and Doreen lined up for the reception at the end of the long great hall at Sanjika, along with the other guests. The Queen entered the hall first, followed by Prince Andrew and the Duke of Edinburgh. "She was beautiful," says Doreen.

"She loved Malawi and was very fond of Dr. Banda." After curtseying or bowing to meet the Queen, the guests, some 200 people, sat down for a grand banquet, "where the President and Queen both made very good speeches," Doreen remarks. The following day, Bruce and Doreen had to get up at the crack of dawn to get back to Lilongwe in time for another reception with the Queen. Together with the British high commissioner, Sir Michael Scott[20], and staff, a private plane was organised to fly them back to Lilongwe. They hurried home, got changed, and drove to the British High Commissioner's residency: "the roads to which were crowded with hundreds and hundreds of people who were all waving". This reception was more intimate than at Sanjika, with a group of only eight people. The High Commissioner informed Bruce and Doreen that Her Majesty would be meeting them first and asked them to stand at the front of the line. This time they were also able to greet Prince Phillip, and, rather wonderfully, we have a photo of Bruce and Prince Phillip conversing.

Another member of royalty who Bruce and Doreen were invited to meet was Princess Anne, who visited Lilongwe as part of her work for the Save the Children charity, in particular to see the Mozambican refugees who had fled the Mozambique civil war in the late 1970s/early 1980s and crossed the border into Malawi. "It started as a trickle, then a flood", Bruce remarks, with an estimated total of 1 million refugees, accounting for 10% of

---

20 Sir Michael Scott was knighted following the Queen's visit. Bruce and Doreen are to this day still in touch with his wife, Jennifer.

Meeting Prince Phillip (1979).

Malawi's population at the time, ended up in Dedza and Mulanje. Bruce and Doreen greeted Princess Anne as she arrived off the plane at Lilongwe airport. Doreen recalls standing next to a young, terribly nervous Malawian girl, who was beautifully dressed up and presented Princess Anne with a bouquet of flowers.

Bruce and Doreen with Princess Anne.

Her Majesty the Queen arriving at Lilongwe airport.

Her Majesty the Queen in Lilongwe.

Other prominent visitors who Bruce and Doreen have had the priviledge of meeting include British Prime Minister Margaret Thatcher, the President of Kenya, Daniel arap Moi, and Kenneth Kaunda, President of Zambia. For Margaret Thatcher a state banquet was held at Sanjika, at which Bruce and Doreen had the fortune of being sat at the table immediately below the stage on which President Banda, Mrs. Thatcher and a few other dignitaries were seated. "Next to us were Margaret Thatcher's foreign advisor and Margaret's press secretary," Bruce explains. For the two Presidents, who visited Malawi on separate occasions, a civic lunch was hosted by the mayor of Lilongwe in their honour.

Below are some of the invites to the aforementioned events:

> Please bring this invitation card with you
>
> *The Provincial Commissioner and Mrs Sharpe request the pleasure of the Company of*
>
> Mr. & Mrs. B.R. Barron
>
> *at a Reception at the Provincial Commissioner's Residence, in honour of Her Majesty Queen Elizabeth, The Queen Mother on Wednesday, the 25th of May, 1960, at 9.45 o'clock a.m.*
>
> R.S.V.P. to the Provincial Commissioner's Office,
> Lilongwe [P.T.O.

> ♛
> **EIIR**
>
> *The British High Commissioner
> is commanded by Her Majesty to invite*
>
> Mr & Mrs B. R. Barron
>
> *to a Reception to be given by
> The Queen and The Duke of Edinburgh
> at the High Commissioner's Residence, Lilongwe
> on Monday, 23rd July, 1979, from 11 a.m.—1 p.m.*
>
> A reply is requested to: ✓
> British High Commission
> Telephone: Lilongwe 731544 Ext. 226
>
> *Dress: Lounge Suit*

An equally prominent event was the Head of State's official birthday, which Bruce was invited to in the 1980s. Bruce received a very formal, enormous printed invitation to the occasion, which was to include a parade to mark the trooping of the Malawi flag, at Kamuzu Stadium in Blantyre. An honour to be invited, Bruce was one of the few people who was given permission to take photos. He stood in the VIP box alongside Major Rickett, the British high commissioner, numerous diplomats and the heads of major companies. The stadium was packed with thousands of Malawians, all dressed in different colours symbolising the different regions they were from. "It was a very splendid affair with military precision," Bruce remarks.

The procession at Dr. Hastings Kamuzu Banda's official birthday.

Dr. Banda's car being driven round Kamuzu stadium as part of the Head of State's official birthday.

Chapter 20: Chairman of Auction Holdings Ltd.

One of the major developments in the 1970s was the President's decision to merge Malawi's two auction floors, Tobacco Auctions and Producers Warehouse (the latter of which Bruce had been a director of, and Mbabzi a major shareholder), to form Auction Holdings Ltd. Bruce explains that because the amount of tobacco being produced had increased so much over the last twenty years or so, the two existing floors were too small to operate the buying of tobacco efficiently.

It was expected that the general manager of ADMARC[21] (the Agricultural Development and Marketing Cooperation), Mr. W. Masiku would become the new chairman of Auction Holdings. It therefore came as a complete shock when Mr. Masiku phoned Bruce to inform him that he was to be the new chairman of Auction Holdings, while Mr. Masiku was to be deputy

---

21 ADMARC was the country's sole grain marketer, and responsible for the marketing of all smallholder crops. A board was set up which included five directors, appointed by ADMARC, and three directors from the minority shareholders, which included Bruce.

chairman. Bruce was told that as this was a presidential order, the appointed job was not something that he could decline.

Being chairman of Auction Holdings was a huge responsibility. Bruce had the task of ensuring the very large organisation, which was responsible for the buying and selling of tobacco for the entire country, ran smoothly and efficiently. The position required a tremendous amount of tact as there were so many conflicting interests, and took up a great amount of Bruce's time. "From the start nearly all the meetings were very difficult and tense and it was a huge strain trying to keep the peace," he says. Luckily, Mr. Masiku, and the general manager, Mr. Ken Robinson, were both very helpful to Bruce and greatly assisted him when they could. Mr. Masiku's successor, Mr. D Z Tembo, also gave great support and encouragement to Bruce, as did Mr. Graham Msonthi, who joined the company from ADMARC as deputy general manager and company secretary. Two other directors who gave Bruce great support were Mr. Hastings Kabambe and Mr. Henry Ntaba.

I ask Bruce for some specifics of the work he was involved in. "One of my major objectives as chairman was localisation," he explains. Training schemes were set up, with the aim of recruiting senior Malawians to the company, to try and disperse the heavy concentration of expats who formed the vast majority of all senior positions. Bruce was told it would take at least five years before the company would have a significant number of trained Malawians working in senior positions. But he proved doubters wrong and two years later there were many senior Malawian employees working for the organisation. "Beyond this it was never to be forgotten that both the growers and the buyers had to see that this one auction floor could cope and smoothly run with the ever increasing size of the crop." Furthermore, the dozens of meetings which took place on a weekly basis were all based in Limbe, which meant Bruce had to drive back and forth from Lilongwe several times a week, again very tiring. "It was one long headache for Bruce," Doreen explains. "It took up a huge amount of time – above and beyond what Mbabzi needed – it was very stressful and a great strain on Bruce".

Bruce explains how "from the beginning I wanted to keep a low profile, if possible, partly by nature and partly to be seen to remain neutral. So I deliberately left the limelight to the general manager as much as I could, i.e. all press interviews, all receiving of VIPs and so forth." However, when Dr. Banda wished to open the auction floors at the start of the tobacco selling season, which occurred on a few occasions, no one else but Bruce's position could receive him and welcome him to the opening. Bruce describes how there would be huge crowds – hundreds of singing and dancing women, most of the cabinet, masses of spectators, police and reporters. Bruce would welcome the President to the opening of the floors, introduce him to the other directors, and once or twice had to make a speech over the radio formally welcoming him. All of this would take time and preparation and added to the responsibility of the role.

OPENING OF ADMARC SHEDS IN PICTURES

Mr. D.Z. Tembo and other officials take the Ngwazi round to visit the Storage Sheds.

Taken from a Malawi newspaper, the photo shows Bruce greeting the *Ngwazi*, "chief of chiefs", President Dr. Banda.

In the late 1970s, the President decided that, following the successful move of all the embassies, government ministries and commercial head offices to Lilongwe, the tobacco headquarters too should do the same. Overseeing the entire move of the auction floors from Limbe to Lilongwe added to the pile of Bruce's responsibilities, requiring endless discussions ranging from how to raise the funds, to the size and layout of the new building, to providing housing facilities for the staff.

The new floors were opened in 1978, at the same time as the new factory of one of Malawi's major buyer companies, Limbe Leaf, was opened. The opening of the auction floors was a fairly low-key affair, with most attention being on the Limbe Leaf factory. However, the opening of the factory turned into an uncomfortable and unpleasant experience; the President first made a verbal attack on the auction floors, calling for Mr. Robinson, the general manager, to come up on the stage. Unfortunately, or perhaps actually rather fortuitously, Mr. Robinson was unwell that day and unable to attend, and so the President called up Jack Stevens, who was the general manager of Limbe Leaf, as well as chairman of ADMARC. Despite having nothing to do with the auction floors, the President publically rebuked Mr. Stevens for the way the auction holdings were being run. Bruce remembers sitting towards the front of the stage, having to listen to this public rebuke, feeling awfully nervous, and praying he would not be called forward. "I was at home listening to all of this on the radio," Doreen adds. "I felt sick with worry, hoping that Bruce would not be mentioned." The President then attacked the ITC, the manager of which, John Bishop, was sat next to Bruce, again publicly humiliating him. Luckily Bruce was not mentioned. Following this, once Ken Robinson was back at work, he and Bruce had to put a plan in place to address the problems that the President had mentioned in his speech, which was another tremendous pressure to deal with.

After a few more years, in 1984, Bruce was finally able to step down as chairman, and Mr. Stevens took over from him. This was a great relief for Bruce as the pressure was taken off him after ten years of dedication, and he was finally able to relax a bit more and devote more attention to the running of the estates.

Unfortunately this didn't last long because in 1988 Mr. Stevens became very ill and was forced to resign. He sadly died soon after. Bruce had been wondering, and dreading, if he would be reappointed again. The call came. Bruce was to go back as chairman of Auction Holdings Ltd. Once again Bruce was inundated with the pressure of making sure the auction floors operated proficiently. Doreen reiterates how all the stress of the job returned: "He really did have the most difficult job. It completely aged him." However, Doreen continues to describe how Bruce's tireless efforts and hard work paid off, as the outcome of his work achieved the respect of everyone in the community and in the tobacco industry. This was made evident when shortly after being re-appointed as chairman, Bruce was asked to also become the chairman of ADMARC, "a great surprise and a tremendous honour". The position at ADMARC was completely non-executive and Bruce and the general manager at the time, Mr. John Magombo, worked together very happily.

Bruce ends the interview session about his responsibilities at Auction Holdings and ADMARC by saying: "When I see what they have both become now, and how they have continued to develop over the years, I feel quite proud of what I did there."

Chapter 21: Busy lives in the 1980s

The mid to late 1970s and 1980s reflect a tremendously busy time for Bruce and Doreen. With both their children in England studying at university and beginning their own lives, Bruce and Doreen's time was filled with commitments, social events, and for Bruce, the continual managing of the three estates. In addition to his responsibilities at Auction Holdings and ADMARC, Bruce had a number of other commitments to adhere to.

These included positions on the boards or organising committees of: Southern Bottlers, in which Mbabzi had large shares; Hogg Robinson (Malawi) Ltd. (insurance brokers); Merchantare Credit (a finance company); the Tobacco Association of Malawi; the Lilongwe Town and Country Planning Committee ("I must have been on this committee for the best part of 25 years"); and the Kasungu Flue Cured Tobacco Authority. Two other important commitments of Bruce were his being a director at the Reserve Bank of Malawi (RBM), the country's central bank, and the founding of Lincoln Investments. For the RBM, the board consisted of a chairman, a few other directors, and a general manager. At the time Bruce was a director, Francis Pelekamoyo was the general manager, who to this day remains on friendly terms with Bruce and Doreen. Another prominent member of the RBM was Mr. Mathews Chikaonda, who, in the early 1990s, served as Deputy Governor, before becoming Governor for five years. Following this Mathews was appointed to the Cabinet and served as Minister of Finance and Economic Planning. Mathews was also appointed as Group Chief Executive of Press Corporation in 2002, and has since become a close business associate of Bruce's son Andrew, who worked with him in his capacity as a director of Press.

It was also around this time that Bruce was advised to set up a separate investment company to hold the Mbabzi interest in the non-agricultural sector, such as its shares in the bottling company, property company, and building companies. So, Bruce set up Lincoln Investments. Bruce continued to put profits into the investment company which slowly expanded and eventually was able to include UK shares. Today it is a well-diversified investment company holding stakes in Malawi businesses as well as having a nice portfolio of UK shares.

Doreen, too, was kept busy by being involved in a range of committees: she was a member of the agricultural society; the Anglican Church PCC; the tennis committee; the Lilongwe hospital advisory committee; the women's association (which was an offshoot of the National Council of Women of which Doreen is still a member of today); and she was still heavily involved in the running of the church fetes.

In addition, and the most interesting of Doreen's commitments, was her appointment to the National Executive of the CCAM, '*Citukuko Cha Amai m'Malawi*' (Women in Development in Malawi). The CCAM was "run by women for women". Notes from Doreen's diary summarises the work that was involved:

"Great strides were taken with President Banda promoting the status of women in the country. Consequently the CCAM was formed. This is an organisation run by women for their development, in the towns and in the most remote villages. Part of CCAM's policy was to send small groups of women overseas to broaden their outlook. This organisation is Malawian but women of other races are invited to join and I am one of about six white women who were invited in the whole country. Public speaking comes high on the agenda, as does etiquette." (Excerpt from Doreen's diary)

On one occasion Doreen recalls receiving a call to rush to the army air wing to meet Mama Kadzamira, the President's official hostess, and a few others. They were to go to Salima to inspect the floods and damage at the local hospital after a recent earthquake: "I remember it being 6.5 on the Richter scale. As soon as we felt the ground shaking your grandfather shot underneath the bed." They travelled by helicopter, with Doreen sat next to Mama, "at which point I realised I must be sat in the President's seat!" On this, and at other events when Mama and Doreen were taking part in CCAM duties, she would give Doreen a large white handkerchief and ask Doreen to wave to the gathered crowds with it.

Every so often the CCAM was invited to an official state reception, where they were asked to welcome the President by singing and dancing, in which Doreen would take part. At one event, the annual convention of the ruling Malawi Congress Party, the ladies had welcomed the President before he addressed his party members. Doreen and the rest of the CCAM were nearby watching him, when suddenly people started muttering to Doreen, and she realised, with shock, that she was being summoned to the stage. The President had started swaying in a dancing fashion, "waving his fly whisk around, which he always had on him during his speeches", and was gesturing for Doreen to dance alongside him, as a special recognition. The ladies of the CCAM started whooping as Doreen joined the stage. "My mind went a complete blank," Doreen exclaims, "as I danced alongside the head of the country in front of the entire Congress Party!"

Amongst all the committees and work commitments, Bruce and Doreen's social lives continued to be busy. There were various tennis courts throughout the region where they would play – Fort Jameson (Chipata), the Lilongwe Golf Club (where they continued to play a lot of golf), the research station at Chitedze, the Nkhoma mission, Dowa and their own courts at Mbabzi. Dowa was particularly social as it was where the headquarters were for the WNLA[22] (the Witwatersrand Native

---

22 The WNLA was created to help recruit Malawians to go and work in the South African mines (this was a major part of the diplomatic ties that bound the President to apartheid South Africa, which virtually no other independent African state recognised).

Labour Association). No.1 house was frequently flowing with visitors, where Doreen would host endless dinner parties, "as often as five nights a week", to entertain the various groups ("the diplomatic crowd", the land development people, Doreen's friends from the CCAM, Mbabzi managers and their families) with whom Bruce and Doreen had become friendly with.

"The 1960s and early 1970s were a period of such change and anxiety, with a lot of stress to deal with. It was a tough period to be white land owners in Africa." Bruce explains. "But the late 1970s and 1980s, overall, were a great time for us – we were both hectically busy, but we enjoyed it immensely."

Doreen explains how the workers who were sent to the mines signed a contract which stipulated that they had to send money back to their families each month. It was a successful initiative which became one of the biggest sources of revenue in Malawi. The organisation had its own planes and pilots which would fly the Malawians to and from Johannesburg. Unfortunately, sometime in the 1970s, one of the WNLA aircrafts carrying mine workers back to Malawi crashed, and the organisation was forced to shut down.

Chapter 22: Handing over

By the mid-1980s both Bruce and Doreen's children had finished their university studies – Elizabeth had completed a degree in French and Italian at Exeter University and Andrew completed a HND in Business Studies at the University of West England in Bristol – and were starting their own lives.

Liz decided to make England her home, where she met and married Chris Randell and began their new life in Uxbridge. She had her first child, Bruce and Doreen's first grandchild, in 1986, christened Sarah after her devoted Malawi nanny of twenty years. Two years later, their second daughter, Victoria, was born. The family moved to Guildford in 1990 where Liz and Chris still live today.

While Liz started married life, and her family, in England, Andrew decided to follow Bruce's footsteps and return to Malawi to work at Mbabzi. While at the University of West England, Andrew met Sheila Dobbs, from North Somerset. They married in 1983 and shortly afterwards, just as Doreen had done with Bruce, Sheila moved out to Malawi with Andrew. They moved into

No.5 house, the first house that their three children, Alexandra, Suzanna and David lived in. All three were born in Malawi (Alex in the Lilongwe Central hospital, and Suzie and David at the Nkhoma Mission hospital, near Dedza).

Three generations of Barrons (from L-R clockwise):
Victoria Randell, Alexandra Barron, David Barron,
Elizabeth Randell, Suzie Barron, Andrew Barron,
Sarah Randell, Doreen Barron, Bruce Barron (2009).

For the first few years Andrew worked under the general manager, Brian Piers, briefly, and then Peter Buttress. In 1989 he formally took over as managing director of Mbabzi – "although I remained very much involved for Andrew's first four years and was able to help him settle into the new job," adds Bruce, who finally gave up the last of his directorships and fully retired in 1993. He and Doreen moved out of No.1 house to No.2 house (a move of less than 500m, across the big lawn). At the same time they bought a nice house in Gerrards Cross, Buckinghamshire in the UK. Today "No.13" in Gerrards Cross has become their more permanent home, with visits to Malawi occurring once or twice a year.

Back at Mbabzi, Andrew's first year as managing director saw the arrival of Michael Kayes (whose wife, Zoe, is Doreen's god-daughter) as the new general manager. Michael and Zoe remained at Mbabzi, living at No.3 house, for 12 years, with Michael proving to be hugely successful and a great asset to Mbabzi.

Since taking full responsibility, Andrew has moved Mbabzi in new directions. In Bruce's time tobacco was by far the most dominant crop, contributing to over 90% of Mbabzi's volumes and earnings. A small amount of groundnuts and maize[23] were also grown. Since then, Mbabzi has greatly diversified and now grows very large quantities of seed maize, commercial maize, and soya beans, as well as groundnuts and sunflower seed, the combination of which currently accounts for 50% of the company's revenue (and tobacco the other 50%). As Bruce states, it was "an enormous achievement to have successfully diversified" from tobacco.

To gather more details on the last 20 years at Mbabzi, I briefly interview Andrew for information, who explains why Mbabzi needed to diversify:

---

23 Maize was not produced on a commercial basis but as food for the tenants.

"When I took over in 1989, Mbabzi was a highly profitable burley tobacco farming operation. However, because of pressure from Western donors, tobacco production was liberalised which meant any farmer could grow tobacco without any crop rotation or necessary land for forestry. This deregulation led to the over production of burley tobacco. Consequently Mbabzi found it difficult to compete with the smallholder farmers, so we had to start looking for alternative crops."

Andrew adds however, that although he introduced these new crops – seed maize, soya, and commercial maize (and to a lesser extent groundnuts and sunflower seed) – he continues to produce tobacco despite prices declining over the years and the industry facing challenges. "Mbabzi also did a brief stint in producing coffee across the estates, but that never paid its way and has now come to an end."

Jan Sinnige, who replaced Michael Kayes in 2001 as general manager of Mbabzi, was instrumental in the introduction of these new crops and continues to ensure their successful production. Previously, Jan had been running Maravi Flowers, which was a joint venture between Mbabzi and some Dutch shareholders. Unfortunately the flower project eventually collapsed because direct flights from Lilongwe to Amsterdam, where the flowers were sold, were cancelled (given the short life of roses, getting them quickly from the ground to the markets in which they are sold is vital).

The soya crop is grown on the left of the track, with tobacco on the right (circa. 2005).

In addition to the crop diversification, other major developments that Andrew has introduced that are important to mention include a tree planting programme, a move towards mechanised production, and the building of a dam up at Monjesi.

The tree-planting programme was started by Bruce, on a small scale, in the 1960s. Cassias were planted on a small acreage on each estate. Bruce also introduced the planting of gmelina, an ant-resistant fairly quick growing tree that could be propagated from seedbeds. These eventually replaced the cassia trees (which were not as resistant to ants and took a lot longer to grow).

When Andrew took over he greatly expanded the acreage of gmelina trees across the estates. Today these trees provide thousands of poles for the hundreds of burley tobacco barns which are needed to cure the tobacco. In addition, a big push was made to plant bamboos. These were planted in long lines across the estates to act as windbreaks, and again are used to build the tobacco barns. The third type of tree planted was the blue gum Eucalyptus, which has proved particularly suitable for planting in marshy areas on the estates in the northern region. Extra wood was also needed to build the very large permanent barns (20ft high by 100ft long with corrugated iron roofs), which Bruce introduced in the 1970s. Over the years Andrew has expanded these, with over 100 large barns being built.

One of the large tobacco barns.

Mechanisation is something which also continues to develop and expand to this day. The majority of the fields today are ploughed by tractor instead of being hand dug by individual tenants with their hoes. As seed maize and soya are primarily grown on a direct labour basis, as opposed to by tenants, this has enhanced the need for mechanisation, with crops being produced using harrowing, planters, spray machines and shellers. The increased mechanisation has led to improved yields, as the preparation of the fields is done far more efficiently than when they are hand-dug. However, despite the increase in machinery, today there are far more employees than there were in Bruce's time. This is due to an extra 1,500 labourers needed to grow all the other crops, aside from tobacco and soya which are grown by the tenants. This is in addition to the 1,000 permanent labourers and 1,000 tenants, and the 500 seasonal graders during peak harvesting times.

A final noteworthy improvement was the dam built on the Monjesi estate in 1995, which provides 500,000 cubic metres of water. "To put it in perspective," Andrew says, "there are 1,000 litres in one cubic metre!" The dam is an enormous asset, providing irrigation for all the crops on the Madisi estate (some 5,000 acres).

Much like Bruce was in his heyday, Andrew is on a number of boards and committees. The most prominent companies he has formal roles in are:

- Auction Holdings Ltd.
- Press Cooperation: the largest corporation in Malawi, owning half of the National Bank of Malawi (the country's largest lender), 42% of Limbe Leaf, half of Carlsberg Coca-Cola, and parts of PTC and Malawi Telecommunications Ltd, among others

- MPICO: the country's largest property company, currently in the process of building the largest shopping mall in Malawi
- Seed-Co Malawi Ltd: Andrew was appointed to the board because of Mbabzi's large involvement in seed production

The Barrons now have six estates: Mbabzi, Monjesi, Valala, Mlamba, (the last two were formerly known as Nyagra, but were split into two estates as Bruce thought it was too big to be managed by one supervisor), Malikha (this was formerly part of the Monjesi estate, which again was split to make managing the land easier) and Kalumbu. The latter is a new estate, based in Mchinji, which was bought in the mid-1990s, where tenant tobacco, seed maize, seed soya, commercial maize, and sunflowers are produced.

Although this chapter has highlighted many changes and new developments, the main things that A.F set up 100 years ago still remain; No.1 house is still standing; the tenant system is still used across the estates; our tobacco is still cured in barns; and the Lilongwe golf club that A.F built still remains the only golf club in Lilongwe. What has also remained over the years are the friends of the Barrons; names of families mentioned throughout the book – Wallaces, Conforzis, Costantinis, Macphersons – all still live and work in Malawi, and are integral parts of the Malawi community.

Who knows what the future holds for Mbabzi – the outlook for British landowners living in Africa is never certain. However, over the last 100 years Malawi has provided us with a home, a livelihood, endless adventures, opportunities and wonderful holidays, spanning across four generations. Bruce ends our final interview session, eight years after the first one, by saying: "The family have been so fortunate to live and work in this wonderful country amongst these wonderful people."

Long may this continue.